I0815242

ANCIENT WISDOM FOR MODERN READERS

▪ ▪ ▪ ▪

For a full list of titles in the series, go to https://press.princeton.edu/series/ancient-wisdom-for-modern-readers.

How to Find Happiness: An Ancient Guide to the Good Life by Marcus Tullius Cicero

How to Be Grateful: An Aztec Guide to the Art of Gratitude by Pablo of Texcoco

How to Cope: An Ancient Guide to Enduring Hardship by Boethius

How to Feel: An Ancient Guide to Minding Our Emotions by the Buddha

How to Be Caring: An Ancient Guide to a Compassionate Life by Shantideva

How to Make a Home: An Ancient Guide to Style and Comfort by Vitruvius and Guests

How to Have Willpower: An Ancient Guide to Not Giving In by Plutarch and Prudentius

How to Talk about Love: An Ancient Guide for Modern Lovers by Plato

How to Eat: An Ancient Guide for Healthy Living by a Buffet of Ancient Authors

How to Lose Yourself: An Ancient Guide to Letting Go by the Buddha and His Followers

How to Be Queer: An Ancient Guide to Sexuality by Sappho, Plato, and Other Lovers

HOW TO BE GRATEFUL

■ ■ ■ ■ ■

An Aztec Guide to the Art of Gratitude

Pablo of Texcoco

Translated and introduced
by Frances Karttunen and Camilla Townsend

PRINCETON UNIVERSITY PRESS
PRINCETON AND OXFORD

Published by Princeton University Press
41 William Street, Princeton, New Jersey 08540
99 Banbury Road, Oxford OX2 6JX

press.princeton.edu

GPSR Authorized Representative: Easy Access System Europe - Mustamäe tee 50, 10621 Tallinn, Estonia, gpsr.requests@easproject.com

ISBN 978-0-691-27411-9
ISBN (e-book) 978-0-691-27412-6

Library of Congress Control Number: 2025942885

British Library Cataloging-in-Publication Data is available

Editorial: Rob Tempio and Chloe Coy
Production Editorial: Karen Carter
Text and Jacket/Cover Design: Heather Hansen
Production: Erin Suydam
Publicity: William Pagdatoon and Charlotte Coyne
Copyeditor: Lachlan Brooks

Jacket image: © Bodleian Libraries, University of Oxford

This book has been composed in Stempel Garamond

Printed in the United States of America

1 3 5 7 9 10 8 6 4 2

Dedicated to the memory of James Lockhart

CONTENTS

ACKNOWLEDGMENTS

The editors are grateful to the Bancroft Library of the University of California, Berkeley, for giving permission to publish this edition of the document they hold, entitled *Discursos Mexicanos, Mexican Manuscript 458*. In 1987, Frances Karttunen together with James Lockhart published an earlier edition, *The Art of Nahuatl Speech: The Bancroft Dialogues*, which included, among other elements, a colloquial translation. Most of that translation is included here with the permission of the UCLA Latin America Institute, for which we offer our deepest thanks. We also want to express our gratitude to our fellow members of the Association of Nahuatl Scholars for their friendship over the

years and for all that we have learned from their valuable work. Rob Tempio and Chloe Coy at Princeton University Press have been the best of editors, and the anonymous reviewers offered helpful advice. Camilla Townsend worked on this project during her time as the Kislak Chair at the Kluge Center of the Library of Congress; she was extremely fortunate to be surrounded by such welcoming staff and colleagues. Tlazocamati huel miac.

A NOTE ON NAHUATL PRONUNCIATION

In reading Nahuatl (or Aztec) words, please keep in mind that the spelling rules for representing Nahuatl sounds were initially devised by Spanish-speaking friars. In a sense, you should approach the words as if you were reading Spanish. The friars recognized four vowels in Nahuatl: a, e, i (which they often wrote as y), and o (which they often wrote as u). They did not understand that there are four short and four long vowels, and they did not make this distinction in spelling. Non-distinction in spelling has carried through to the present. The Nahuatl vowels are pronounced more or less as they are in these Spanish words:

a as in *casa*, "house"
e as in *el*, "the"
i as in *ir*, "to go"
o as in *ojo*, "eye" (with the long vowel apparently sounding to the friars more like u as in *un*, "one")

In old Spanish the letter x was used to represent the initial consonant of English *shoe*. A sound change has taken place in Spanish with the x spelling becoming archaic, but x in Nahuatl retains the English sh pronunciation: so we have Nahuatl *xoctli* ("pot") and *textli* ("flour").

In English spelling, pairs of letters are sometimes used to represent single consonants, such as sh in words like *shoe* and *hush* and th in words like *this* and *with*. English, Spanish, and Nahuatl all use the pair of letters ch to repre-

sent the sound as in English *church*, Spanish *chucho* ("dog"), and Nahuatl *chichi* ("dog"). Likewise, the friars resorted to combinations of letters to represent some Nahuatl consonants that do not occur in Spanish. The most ubiquitous of these sounds is the one written as tl, which represents a single t-sound made to one side of the tongue. In this way, it is different from the sound of English words like *bottle*, where the t and l are pronounced separately.

Spanish uses the pair of letters hu to represent the sound that is written w in English: Spanish *hueso* ("bone"). In Nahuatl this consonant can appear both before and after vowels. For the most part the friars reversed the order of the letters when the w-sound follows a vowel: Nahuatl *hual-* ("hither") versus *auh* ("and"). (This switch actually reflects the fact that this w-consonant

is softened in pronunciation after vowels.) Likewise, although Spanish and Nahuatl share a sound represented by cu as in Spanish *cual* ("which"), Nahuatl also has this consonant after vowels, where the friars reversed the spelling: Nahuatl *cual* ("good") and *iuctli* ("younger brother or sister"). Confusingly, they sometimes spelled this single Nahuatl consonant with three letters: cuh as in *icuhtli*, inviting mispronunciation as a whole extraneous syllable.

Two other consonants need to be mentioned: a consonant that Nahuatl does not share with Spanish is written tz both before and after vowels: for example, Nahuatl *tzictli* ("chicle," "chewing gum") and Tetzcohco, the Nahuatl name of the Mexican city of Texcoco. Lastly, Nahuatl has a consonant that occurs in the English exclamation for when something goes wrong: *oho!* (or "uh-oh!"). This consonant, called a glottal stop,

is made by snapping the vocal cords closed for an instant. The friars were somewhat aware of this consonant and sometimes wrote it with the letter h. Mostly they omitted it completely.

Finally, in Nahuatl the stress is always on the next to last syllable except when a man (but not a woman) directly addresses another person. In this one case, the male vocative, the stress is on the final syllable. Women express the vocative by means of a high tone on the final syllable.

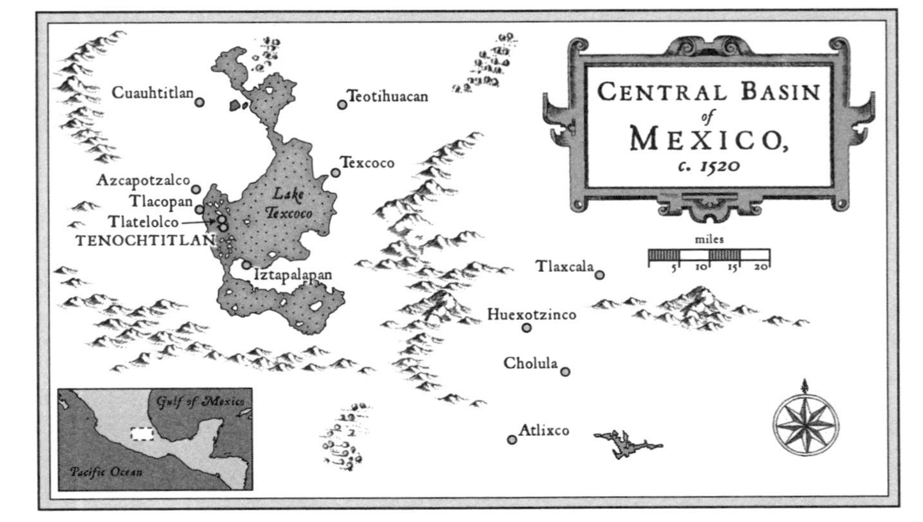
CENTRAL BASIN
of
MEXICO,
c. 1520
miles
5
10
15
20
Cuauhtitlan
Teotihuacan
Texcoco
Azcapotzalco
Tlacopan
Tlatelolco
TENOCHTITLAN
Lake Texcoco
Iztapalapan
Tlaxcala
Huexotzinco
Cholula
Atlixco
Gulf of Mexico
Pacific Ocean

INTRODUCTION

One mid-sixteenth-century day, a Nahuatl (or Aztec)-speaking woman stopped by to visit some family members on her way to market. She was a lady of a high-ranking Indigenous family in the town of Texcoco, Mexico. Some fifty years earlier, her immediate ancestors had been governing figures in what is now called the Aztec Triple Alliance. The elders on whom she was paying a call were likewise important people, and so she spoke to them in a polite and formal register intended to convey her respect for them as well as her gratitude for all they had done in their younger years.

Not long after, an Indigenous man named Pablo who happened to be present sat down and

wrote what he could recall of the exchanges between the generations. At first, he was recording a real event. But soon his quill pen took flight, and he began to write down other verbal exchanges that he had heard or read or imagined. He created a text that would ultimately convey to future generations the values of his people and the mental world they inhabited, one that revolved around gratitude to past generations and expectations of future ones. Although written in the 1500s, when Europeans were present, his work nevertheless harkens back to earlier times in Indigenous America.[1]

Texcoco and the Aztec World

Texcoco has sometimes been called the "Athens" of preconquest Mesoamerica, both because of the beautiful architecture and gardens later described

by the Spaniards ("half in the water and half on land") and because of the people's purported love of poetic songs.[2] At the time that Pablo lived there, the city already had a deep history.[3] The Acolhua people were an ethnic group that had long farmed and fished on the east side of a great lake that filled much of the central basin of Mexico. By the 1300s, they had established a range of interrelated *altepetl*, or city-states, the most powerful of which was Texcoco. However, in the wider world, Texcoco was not dominant: the people of Texcoco were forced to pay tribute to the more powerful Tepaneca people on the west side of the lake, and Texcoco's ruler had been pressured to add a Tepaneca wife to his household and make her children his heirs.

In the 1420s, a political crisis occurred. The high king of the Tepaneca died, triggering a civil war among his various sons by different

mothers. One group in particular quickly took advantage of the chaotic situation: the Mexica people—often known to us today as the Aztecs—lived on an island in the center of the lake, in an altepetl called Tenochtitlan, and they had their own troublesome internal divisions. One branch of the Mexica royal family immediately formed an alliance with the branch of the Tepaneca royal family that seemed to be losing the war and thus welcomed allies. The Mexica leader Itzcoatl (Obsidian Snake) also made overtures to a prince of Texcoco who had been ousted from the line of inheritance because his mother wasn't Tepaneca, and he happily joined the group of outsiders-on-the rise. He took the name Nezahualcoyotl (Hungry Coyote). Together, the three groups (the Tepaneca from a place called Tlacopan, the Mexica under Itzcoatl, and the people of Texcoco under Neza-

hualcoyotl) attained a great victory and founded a cooperative ruling alliance that scholars today often refer to as the Aztec Triple Alliance. For the next century, they controlled most of central Mexico and sought to control lands to the north, south, and east. They collected tribute from far and wide and waged deadly war against those who opposed them.[4]

Nezahualcoyotl became a great ruler. He governed for over fifty years, transforming Texcoco into a handsome metropolis and hosting great fetes where the people drummed and danced and sang far into the night. When he died in his seventies, he had dozens of children by multiple wives. After some skirmishing and some political negotiations, it was eventually agreed that his nine-year-old son by a sister of the current Mexica ruler would inherit.[5] The boy's promoters gave him the apt name of Nezahualpilli (a construction

that in effect means "Child of Nezahualcoyotl"). Nezahualpilli also ruled for decades, and continued his father's tight connection with the Mexica ruling family, as the Triple Alliance rendered Texcoco's people rich and powerful, second only to the Mexica themselves.

Nezahualpilli died in 1515, and this time, the bitter arguments between different sets of brothers by different mothers proved harder to control. From the time that Moteuczoma (who would soon become world famous) came to power in the early 1500s, he had been working hard to replace Nezahualpilli's accepted heirs with a child named Cacama (Small or Secondary Ear of Maize), a baby born to Nezahualpilli by Moteuczoma's own niece. But this was not easy to do, for Texcoco's former heirs consisted of a band of seven sons, all born to one mother and with great mutual loyalty. When Nezahualpilli died, a

civil war broke out, and eventually Texcoco was split in two, with half ruled by Cacama, now an adolescent, and half by the previously accepted heirs. The ruler of the latter half was called Coanacochtli, and a brother named Ixtlilxochitl (Black-Eyed Flower) was his war chief. (Flowers often symbolized warriors, with their perfect beauty and their vulnerability to rapid death.)[6]

When the Spaniards in the expedition of Hernando Cortés arrived, they soon learned that the political geography of Mexico was complex, and they recognized that this might prove useful to them. Many city-states resented the power of the Triple Alliance and became increasingly interested in joining the Spaniards, especially when they found that the Europeans' ships, horses, metal armor, and long-range crossbows rendered the newcomers remarkably effective in battle. Still, Texcoco was tightly allied to the

Mexica and had a great deal to lose if the Triple Alliance fell, so they did not run to join the outsiders. First Cacama and later Coanacochtli made their way to Tenochtitlan to take a stand at the side of the Mexica.[7]

However, the war chief Ixtlilxochitl saw an opportunity for himself and his band of full brothers and so he proceeded differently. He approached the Spaniards, engaged in lengthy conversations through a translator, and soon converted to Christianity. He even agreed to marry one of his wives in a Christian ceremony. The Spaniards were delighted, and even more so when Ixtlilxochitl brought several of his royal brothers and many of their warriors to fight as allies of the Europeans. When the newcomers went to Texcoco to seal the deal, however, they found that it was harder to convince all

of the ordinary people of Texcoco to come over to their side than Ixtlilxochitl had claimed it would be: "In all their streets and houses," remembered one of the Spaniards, "we didn't see any women or young people or children, but rather that all the Indian [men] seemed stunned and ready to fight."[8] However, Ixtlilxochitl did manage to bring enough of the doubting men of Texcoco to fight against their old Mexica allies to make a significant difference; he also allowed the strangers to build ships on the shores of the lake, in which they could rapidly bear down on the island city of Tenochtitlan. In exchange, the Europeans supported the claims to rulership of Ixtlilxochitl's family. Unsurprisingly, Ixtlilxochitl's descendants remembered for many years the brilliant role he had played in the otherwise potentially destructive war and in restoring the

Texcoco royal line to power. His great-great-grandson wrote:

> Afterwards [when the war had ended], Ixtlilxochitl returned to his city of Texcoco, where he was welcomed. He found the entire city sacked and ruined by [their enemies] the Tlaxcalteca. He had everything cleaned and repaired, especially the palaces of his father and grandfather [Nezahualpilli and Nezahualcoyotl] and those of other lords. . . . He gave out many rewards to all the lords, captains and soldiers who fought in his army in support of the Christians, especially those who had distinguished themselves in battle. He ordered the Mexica whom he brought from Mexico—he had personally captured almost two thousand of them—to build great houses and palaces at the place called

> Tecpilpan. His father had given him the town as a child, and he grew up there. He ordered all his vassals there to always be prepared with everything they might need in case of war or emergency.[9]

Unfortunately, Indigenous allies did not retain as much control over the situation as they held at first. Not long after the Spaniards' victory over the Mexica in 1521, Ixtlilxochitl found himself trying to prevent the Spaniards from killing his beloved brother Coanacochtli, as his strategy had differed from Ixtlilxochitl's and he had answered to the Mexicas' call and had fought at their side in Tenochtitlan. Ixtlilxochitl was only able to stave off his brother's execution for a few years. Later, he himself ruled Texcoco. When in 1531 he began to use violence in defending the Texcoco altepetl's landholdings

in the face of depredations by local Spaniards, the high court arrested him and deposited him in a prison cell maintained by the Franciscans in Mexico City. There, he grew seriously ill. They brought him back to Texcoco, but he died shortly after.[10] Nevertheless, by that time, he had helped his people negotiate the chaos of the early years of Spanish rule, preparing them to maintain many aspects of their lives much as they always had been.

Pablo of Texcoco

Pablo worked on his writing project about his people's way of thinking somewhere between the 1550s and the 1570s. That is to say, he lived at least one full generation after the Spanish invasion, and possibly two. In his text, it is the very old who have clear memories of what life

was like before the arrival of the strangers from across the sea, and that would have been the case in his real life as well. But younger people also still lived very much within a Nahua frame of reference: at that point, only a relatively small minority had learned to speak Spanish, and so older ways of thinking were still dominant.[11]

Christianity was indeed spreading during Pablo's youth. Because Texcoco was such an important altepetl, it was one of the first places where the newly arrived Franciscan friars established a mission. There, in the 1520s, the friars began to teach the sons of leading families alphabetic writing, in order that they might better study Christian texts and help to convert their brethren. In 1536, the Franciscans founded a school at Tlatelolco, the altepetl on the northern edge of Tenochtitlan's island, with the intention of bringing pupils from Indigenous noble families all over

Mexico. Many of the young students proved to be brilliant scholars, and they worked together with their friar-teachers to produce important texts in Nahuatl—confessionals, sermonaries, religious plays, and the like.[12] Soon a printing press was able to produce dozens of copies of these for the clergy to use in their work. Fray Alonso de Molina, working with Indigenous aides, created an extraordinary Spanish-Nahuatl / Nahuatl-Spanish dictionary. In the 1550s, '60s, and '70s, one of the teachers, fray Bernardino de Sahagún, worked on a grand ethnographic project in which elders were interviewed on a wide range of topics and their responses were transcribed. It is virtually certain that someone close to Pablo attended the school at Tlatelolco, because one part of his text was actually copied from the pages of the encyclopedia project, with only minor variations.[13]

Yet despite the familiarity of someone in Pablo's world with the Franciscan project, we should not imagine that Pablo was someone who had been overwhelmingly influenced by Christianity, to the extent that he had lost sight of his own culture. That was not the case. Alphabetic writing was by now being taught within the Nahua community, so some young people were learning to use it without any direct teaching from European friars. This shows in the text, where the author writes the name "Pablo" the way he heard it as a Nahua accustomed to his own language: "Papolo." Like many other Nahuas, he used alphabetic writing to carry out projects that the original Franciscan teachers knew nothing about. Some Nahuas employed it, for instance, to transcribe traditional historical performances, songs, and occasionally even prayers.[14] That is, they used the alphabet to sound out and write down words

in their own language, so that the old oral texts would never be lost. Their people had long had their own glyphic writing system, but those symbols were largely mnemonic devices for expert speakers. The people who were trained to interpret the glyphs were fast disappearing, and the young people were well aware of this. In short, although the Nahuas were employing an alphabet that came from the Mediterranean region in the Old World, they often did so for their own purposes. It is certainly true that sometimes they demonstrated clear Christian influence in their writings, but sometimes they simply wrote down what Nahua elders—who spoke no Spanish and knew little of Spanish culture—wished them to record. Pablo's work demonstrates that he could and would do either.[15]

Pablo himself lived very much within the Nahua world. At home in Texcoco, Pablo was

trained in the Nahua art of rhetoric, meaning that he was hired to play a key role in weddings and other important ceremonies. Even today, weddings in Nahuatl-speaking villages in Mexico still contain segments of traditional exhortations by trained speakers. "When your children grow up, what are you going to do with them?" demands the speaker. "You are going to give them the same advice we give you now, advice that was given to us by our parents. Now you have heard me."[16] In the mid-1500s, this verbal artform still remained largely unchanged from what it had been fifty years earlier, before the arrival of the Europeans.

We must emphasize that "Pablo" may have been a pseudonym of sorts. The original writer of the dialogues did not sign his name—which was typical of Nahuas at that time, as they tended to see their work as communal, in the way that

the traditional oral genres had always been communal. But in the text itself, it is a character named "Pablo" who, as a trained speaker, repeatedly takes responsibility for leading the oral exchanges. Even if this was simply a name invented for the purposes of the text, it is fitting that we use it to refer to the man in question: in the preconquest world, Nahuas often changed their names as they proceeded through life and new experiences yielded new monikers.[17] (The up-and-coming ruler who took the metaphorical name "Hungry Coyote," for instance, was not called that as an infant.) There is a real possibility that Pablo, despite all his talent in the art of rhetoric, was not equally gifted in the art of writing; conceivably, it was some other friend or connection of his who did the actual writing. Even if that is the case, however, that person should not be considered the author of

the work, merely the transcriber. The one who created the dialogues—the original, oral text—was the figure who at least in some contexts went by the name of Pablo.

Outline of Pablo's Dialogues

The dialogues that Pablo produced contain thirteen subsections written in Nahuatl, laid out and labeled in Spanish by some later editor. However, if we ignore the many imposed divisions and read the work through as a whole, we see that the dialogues ultimately constitute three distinct parts, each one of which renders the other two more meaningful. The author moves back and forth between generations of the present, the past, and then the present again, allowing them almost to speak to each other. People in the 1560s or '70s harken back to the 1490s or early 1500s,

seeking guidance and expressing gratitude, and the remembered figures of bygone days speak meaningfully to posterity, conveying their expectation that as people of the past, they will be appreciated. It is even said that the people of the past are grateful to those of the present for protecting the future.

The author opens in his own time, in the mid-sixteenth century, with a scene so prosaic that it can only have been inspired by a real event: a woman pays a call on some older relatives as she goes to market. Their high-register language is then reflected in a more formal scene, a wedding, in which Pablo is the speaker who addresses each of the relevant parties: the young people who are marrying, their parents, and the Indigenous governor and his council, who are responsible for the community as a whole.

Then suddenly the author moves backward in time, to the era of the parents or grandparents who once educated him—to the time of people who were born before the Spaniards came. This is the part where the author had recourse to materials that had been gathered in the 1550s by the team of students who worked with fray Bernardino de Sahagún. Once again, we hear elaborate speech exchanges at a marriage, but this time, the emissaries of a preconquest Texcoco lord are visiting the Mexica city of Tenochtitlan to secure a bride for their lord. (It is a complicated situation, because the girl is herself the product of a Mexico-Texcoco union, as interfamilial marriage alliances among noble clans often extended back for generations.)[18] The young woman returns with the marriage brokers to Texcoco, and her husband-to-be welcomes her warmly. Then a skilled speaker once again

addresses the various constituencies. Everyone hopes that the young bride will bear children. She soon does, and the speaker praises her. Eventually, the old lord dies and the speaker leads the people in their mourning. But all will yet be well, we learn, for the old ruler has fathered children who will lead the people forward into the future.

Now the author returns to the present. We come to understand that the old lord was actually Ixtlilxochitl (Black-Eyed Flower, whom we met earlier in this introduction), son of Nezahualpilli and grandson of Nezahualcoyotl: the author records speech exchanges between two of the old lord's direct descendants (two mischievous boys), their tutor, their young mother, and some elderly relatives. The adults discuss what the boys know and compare it to what they *should* know. An aging grandmother figure recalls how children were educated when

she was a child, in the 1490s and early 1500s, before the Spaniards had ever been heard of. She tells some racy stories about those days—stories that other existing sources seem to confirm. (For instance, she recalls one of the ways in which Nezahualpilli was pressured to dishonor the mother of one of his earlier heirs, to make way for Cacama, child of the current Mexica ruler.)[19] The old woman claims there have been sad changes since the days of her youth. Yet what is important has lasted, as becomes clear when a group of singers come to perform for the current Indigenous governor of Texcoco and they exchange classic high-brow greetings and offer him a very old song that delights him.[20] Even though the attitude of the two particular young boys may leave something to be desired, the people of the present have not forgotten to appreciate the people of the past.

The Messages of the Text

Pablo's dialogues make two very different sets of points. On the one hand, they serve the purposes of the Christian friars in late sixteenth-century Mexico; but on the other, they capture and convey a Nahua cultural framework that the Nahua writer fervently wished to preserve for posterity.

In the mid-sixteenth century, the Franciscans and other religious orders were caught up in the project of teaching the Christian faith through texts written in vernacular languages, rather than leaving its works solely in Latin, which was inscrutable to almost everyone except priests and friars. In this, they were influenced by the spirit of Protestantism—the notion that believers should have a direct connection to God—that was sweeping through Europe. As the years went by, however, the Church turned against this movement and began to shut down such projects in

order to reassert the authority of highly trained priests.[21] But Pablo lived in the movement's heyday, when the Franciscans were still eagerly collecting linguistic and ethnographic material for use in proselytizing. The nature of the text itself makes it evident that there had been some sort of assignment—or at least a request—that someone prepare copious dialogues that illustrated the Nahuas' elaborate conversational conventions, and specifically, what was called *huehuetlatolli* ("ancient discourse").[22] From the earliest years after the conquest, the friars had attempted to study the phenomenon of this courtly style of speech, a genre that was generally employed to lecture to younger adults learning their roles in society.[23] The Spaniards seemed fascinated by the Nahuatl-language rhetorical tradition, probably partly because the high-flown speeches could be compared to those of the classical world they

knew so well, and partly because the beautiful phrases were themselves intrinsically compelling. There can be no question that teaching through imaginary dialogues was an old tradition in Europe, but not so far as we know in the Aztec world; this fact alone surely constitutes evidence that the original impetus for the project came from an outsider.

The influence of European thought shows in other ways as well. Although the text uses some pre-contact terms for the divine, it employs them only to allude to a single all-powerful god, which would not have been the case in earlier generations. The editors have chosen to use an initial capital in "our Lord" to convey clearly that the text is referring to the Christian concept of God. Likewise, when the children are told to pray before eating, we are probably seeing a reference to a table prayer that was included

in early Nahuatl catechisms written by Franciscans. On the other hand, there is relatively little evidence of deeply internalized Christian concepts, at least not those that are profoundly different from prior beliefs. The idea that humanity is entirely in God's hands is indeed Christian, but the comparable belief that humans have no power whatsoever over the will of the divine is also a key concept in the oldest Nahuatl-language song lyrics.

It was Pablo's own imagination and the cultural traditions that he knew so well that ultimately shaped the dialogues into the work of art that they became. He had clearly received a Christian name through baptism, and his Franciscan interlocutor may have been most interested in linguistic exposition and forms of rhetoric, but he himself wanted to convey how people were taught to appreciate and respect each other as well as the gifts of the

divine. He wished to demonstrate what succeeding generations should appreciate in each other. Over and over hearers are told that they will be loved and honored if they exert themselves and do their utmost to repay those who have always worked on their behalf—be they living parents and family members or the ancestors of the past. They should do this by doing their duty by their people and making their future viable—by "paying it forward," as we would say today. Life on earth is hard, they thought, and there is very little room for selfishness if humans are to avoid disaster. Future generations will thank them for their efforts, as they must be grateful to those who have gone before.

Naturally, the Nahuas expressed the concept of gratitude in their own way. If readers consult the Nahuatl passages on the left-hand pages of this edition, they will not find any words

that translate literally and directly to our noun "gratitude" or our verb "to thank." Yet these concepts are everywhere implicitly: speakers constantly refer to the act of receiving something as enjoying it, deserving it, being so lucky to get it, and so on. And the idea also appears in specific phrases that are simply different than the ones we use: the most pervasive formulation consists of the phrase "you have befriended me" (from the verb *icnēliā*). On the very first folio, the sentence that literally reads, "You have befriended us [by visiting]" (*ōtitēchmocnēlilih*), we choose to translate as "We thank you [for visiting]," as that is what the writer meant in the terms that an English speaker would use. In another example, the naughty boys' tutor speaks on their behalf to an elder, likewise saying, "You have befriended your grandchildren" (*ōtiquinmocnēlilih*, f.9r), which in

effect translates as, "Your grandchildren thank you." The next most frequent formulation of the concept is "for someone's heart to deliver [or grant] [non-specific] things" (*tlacāhua -yōllohtzīn*). After eating a delicious meal, one of the boys says, "The heart of our Lord has granted things" (*ōtlacāuhqui in īyōllohtzīn*, f.12r) meaning in effect "Our Lord has been generous" or in the words we would use, "I give thanks to our Lord." A third formulation of the concept of gratitude is "to acknowledge as dear, as valuable" (*tlazohcāmati*). In the dialogues we find one instance of this: "I acknowledge as very dear your inquiry, your greeting" (*cencah nictlazohcāmati in motēcatlahtlaniliz in motēciauhquetzaliz*, f.13r), or as we might say, "I greatly appreciate them" or "I thank you for them." Though it is rare in this text, it is this form that ended up surviving

the decades: *Tlazocamati* is used today among Nahuatl speakers to express "thank you."[24]

For many of us living in the secular modern and non-Native world, this emphasis on gratitude to others may feel quite alien. For us, most often, attaining wisdom is understood to consist of honing one's own perspective or learning to defend the self that we envision or wish to become. Sometimes wisdom is also understood to consist of learning to recognize another person's (or group's) perspectives or vision of themselves. But here we find something quite foreign to either project: here, attaining wisdom is about learning to understand oneself as a small part of a greater interdependent whole, not only of a community of living people, but also of a collectivity constituted across generations. The Nahuas probably were not wrong to value this concept. Today's psychologists are beginning to

argue that we have made a mistake in modern times in letting the idea of gratitude recede, and that we should do more to develop it.[25]

Perhaps fortunately for us modern readers, Pablo's dialogues are not purely serious and pious conversations that express values quite different than our own. Like many of the Nahuas of his time, Pablo delighted in interesting metaphors and wry humor. (How he loved the juxtaposition of the flowery language leading up to such mundane moments as two grubby boys thanking their mom for a snack!) He was, in short, profoundly different from us in some ways, and startlingly similar in others.

The History of the Text

Pablo's dialogues were probably well thumbed by the Franciscan or Franciscans who requested

them and were certainly treasured by them. We say this because years later, a man from another order was made aware of their existence and asked to see them. This was father Horacio Carochi, a linguistically gifted Jesuit who ultimately wrote the greatest grammar of classical-era Nahuatl that we have. An Indigenous aide of his who is identified only as "don Miguel" copied out the text, this time inserting markers of distinctive vowel length and segmental glottal stops for which the Jesuits were in the process of developing a system of representation. Don Miguel's copy is in fact the only early version of the dialogues to survive to modern times.[26]

The small set of folios on ordinary European paper measures twenty-three centimeters in height. Someone treasured this copy for many years, and in the nineteenth century, the document passed into the hands of Mexican

historian José Fernando Ramírez (1804–1871). Because he sided with the losers in a civil war,[27] he was forced to flee to Europe, where he ended up selling much of his collection. The dialogues and other items were purchased by Hubert Howe Bancroft (1832–1918), whose collection was sold to the University of California in 1905. The document resides today at the Bancroft Library of UC Berkeley (accessioned as MSS Mexican Manuscript 458).[28] At mid-century, photocopies of most (but not all) of the dialogues were sent to a literary scholar in Mexico, father Angel María Garibay, and he published them in the Nahuatl studies journal *Tlalocan* in 1943.

Then in the 1980s, in the midst of a great florescence of Nahuatl studies in the United States, linguist Frances Karttunen worked with historian James Lockhart to prepare a com-

plete transcription and English translation of the entire work (including a literal translation as well as a colloquial one). They published their edition in 1987 as *The Art of Nahuatl Speech: The Bancroft Dialogues*. The volume included linguistic analysis of the work's rhetorical style and categories, vocabulary, orthography, and diacritics. Readers who wish to research those topics should begin by consulting that work.[29]

Now, forty years later, we present a new edition of the text, underscoring the role of the Texcoco author and the cultural values he wished to record. Pablo's work is particularly valuable to us because it comes packaged in a genre or format that is familiar to us, and yet presents largely pre-contact Nahua values without extensive manipulation by the friars. Many other pieces produced in response to friars' queries sound more like whatever the Indigenous imagined they

were supposed to say, whatever the friars wished to hear.[30] And other pieces produced without the involvement of any Europeans were written in unfamiliar genres that modern readers would find opaque.[31] Don Pablo's voice speaks loud and clear across the centuries, just as he hoped would be the case.

Notes on Transcription and Translation

Frances Karttunen has transcribed the text as it appears in the surviving seventeenth-century Jesuit copy, in which pronunciation was faithfully recorded. Some readers of the language may not be familiar with the diacritics the Jesuits had come to employ in order to represent distinctive vowel lengths: a straight line over a vowel (a macron) indicates a long sound, while no line

indicates a short sound. These differences in pronunciation are very important, as they can disambiguate distinct words. Here is an example where it makes such a difference:

achtli (short vowel): seed
āchtli (long vowel): elder brother [of a younger sister]

Sometimes, but not usually, the copyist of this text introduced one further diacritic, a breve, to redundantly mark short vowels, rather than relying on the absence of a marker, like this:

ăchtli: seed (same as above)

The Jesuits had also developed the system of using a downward slanting line (a grave) over a vowel to indicate that a glottal stop would follow. This is the same consonant that others often

represent as an h in their renderings of Nahuatl. Here is an example:

> àço (instead of *ahzo*): perhaps

Occasionally, the copyist used a circumflex for a glottal stop at the end of a sentence:

> *in titeòpouhquê*: we the afflicted (meaning "we mortals")

The use of these diacritics reveals a great deal about the pronunciation of classical-era Nahuatl, which in turn has helped to deepen our understanding of the words of the language and their construction.[32]

The manuscript gives evidence of the copyist occasionally changing his mind about the best pronunciation, or being corrected by another hand, but in this book, we have included only the copyists' final decision. In addition, we have

sometimes inserted in brackets a letter or two that the copyist seems to have accidentally omitted, or that we can't quite read, but can tell from context must have been intended. All other errors or mysterious elements are commented upon in the notes.

Our translations are derived from the literal meanings of the sentences, but we most often give the most colloquial English translation possible, so that it will not appear that the sixteenth-century Nahuas thought about things very strangely. They simply had their own manner of expressing themselves, as we discussed earlier in our section about their ways of speaking of what we call "gratitude." Occasionally, we have included more literal translations, when it has seemed to us that a particular metaphor or image being employed deserves to be seen by modern readers because it affects the meaning in

an important way or is especially illuminating of Nahua thinking. For instance, when they called their children their "jeweled necklaces," we translate their words literally, rather than writing, "I deeply value you." Some readers may wish to see more of the literal meanings than we have shown, and we urge them to consult the literal translation that was published in 1987.[33]

Nahuatl is a marvelous language, with clever and often unexpected ways of handling certain grammatical phenomena. Today, there are numerous avenues for studying Nahuatl, either the modern variety still spoken by over a million people, or the classical-era form, accessible in books and language courses. Newcomers to the field will find that they have a world of discovery awaiting them.[34]

HOW TO BE GRATEFUL

Saludacion de una, que yendo al tianguez passa por casa de sus parientes.

Tlā ximēhuiltìtiecan nocihuāpiltzin, namēchonnomòcihuiliz* ca çan nican amopantzinco niquīztēhua amocatzinco nitlàtlantiquiça, àço tepitzin anquimomàcēhuìtzinoà, in ītēchicāhualiztzin in tlācatl in totēcuiyo, ca ye īxquich cāhuitl in in aoquīc amīxtzinco amocpactzinco nitlachia, ca yè inic ōnihuāllà in nichuāltepotztoca tiānquiztzīntli, canel tiuhquè in ticŏcoquè in titeòpouhquê.

---

* Carochi's copyist Martín inserted the following: "Aqui es mas usado, namēchonnàmanilīz." He continued to make other occasional comments, but we will not include all of them.

PART I

The Present[1]

Greeting of a woman who passes by the house of her relatives on the way to market.

Do stay seated, my lady. I (don't wish to)[2] disturb you, for I'm just passing by your place here to ask about you, whether you are enjoying a bit of the health of our Lord,[3] for it's been a while since I've seen your faces. What I have come about is to look into things at the market, for so it is with us who are afflicted (us ordinary mortals).[4]

Resp[a]

Oticmìhiyōhuiltì noconētzin notlaçòichpōchtzin, ca mochāntzinco in otimocalaquīco: cuix titechmotlànēhuilia? auh ōtitechmocnēlilì, ca achìtzin tēchmochicāhuilia in tlācatl in totēcuiyo, ca tepitzin tontzōmōcnemì in ītlālticpactzīnco. Çan nō ĭhui in tèhuātzin, ihuan in nohuèpōltzin in pīpiltzitzintin tiquinmotlănēhuìtzinoa, cuix nō tepitzin quinmochicāhuilia in īpalnemoalōni? cuix nocè itlà ītēmŏxtzin ièēcatzin īmpan quihuālmihuālia? Mācihui izçan nican, ca achi onānticatqui; quēnin huel toconmatizquè inic mitzmòtlatoctilia in tlācatl in totēcuiyo?

Nocihuāpiltzin ōtinechmocnēlili, ca nō tepitzin tocontomàcēhuià in ītēchicāhualiztzin in tlŏquè nāhuăquè, ca mopāquiltìticà in mohuèpōltzin, ihuan in mocnōtlăcăhuan pīpiltotōntin ca pāctinemì: ōtoconmìtalhuì, mācihui izçan nican, ca ăchi onānticatqui, ca yè inic tamēchontoxic-

Reply.

Greetings, my child, my dear daughter. You have entered your home; will you stay a while? And thank you, yes, our Lord is keeping us somewhat healthy, and somehow we are scraping along on His earth. And is the Giver of life[5] also keeping you and my brother-in-law and the children whom you have for a time[6] a bit healthy likewise? Or has he sent some illness down upon them? Although it is here (in the general vicinity), it is quite a distance (from your house to ours). How are we to know how our Lord is causing you to fare?

Response of the woman on her way to the market.

Thank you, my lady, we too enjoy a bit of the health of the All-pervasive; your brother-in-law is in good health, and your humble servants, the

cāhuilia in àmo amocatzinco tihuāllà[t]lănì: mā xitēchmotlapòpolhuilīcān in īxpantzīnco in tlācatl in totēcuiyo.

[f.1v] *Despidese la que va al tianguez.*

Tlă oc ximocēhuìtzinōcān, ca ye namēchnotlāl-cāhuilia, tlă oc nontiānquĭçò, àco* huel oc ceppa amopantzīnco nonquīztēhuaz: mā totēcuiyo amēchmopieli.

R[a.]

Mā moyōlīcàtzin, ōtitēchmocnēlilì, in topampa timàāquiltìtihuītz: mā ītlà timitztŏcxināmictilìtin: mā totēcuiyo mitzmohuīquili.

---

* There is a cedilla missing here, a rare mistake in this text.

little children, are healthy. You said that though it is here (in the vicinity), it is quite a distance (from your house to ours). That's why we neglect you and don't come to ask about you. Forgive us, before our Lord.[7]

The woman going to the market takes her leave.

Stay at rest (don't get up). I'm leaving you now. After I've been at the market, it could be I'll come by your place again; may our Lord keep you.

Reply.

Take it easy now. Thank you for having come entering here on our account, don't let us detain you. May our Lord guide you.

Para bien a unos casados.

Ō, noxōcoyōhuāne ōamechmocnēlilī in tlācatl in totēcuiyo, auh in tonāntzin in Xanta yclexia in techmotquilia in techmomāmālia, inic ōamechmolpilì inic ōamechmocētililì, mā ihuiān, mā yōcoxca xonmohuīcatihuian xonmoyacantihuian: mā onixtlāhui mā ompōpōhui in ìhiyōtzin in ȳtlàtōltzin in īpalnemoani in īteōyōtzin in ōamēchmāxcātilì in ōamechmonemactilì. Mā īxquich amotlàpal xoconmochīhuilīcān nopilhuāne: mā xicmotlayecoltilīcān in amoteōtzin in amotlàtòcātzin: mānēn anmoxiccauhtin, mānēn tōchtli maçātl iòhui anquitocatin: mā anmotepèxihuìtì, mā anmātōyāhuìtì. In tèhua in titlàpaltzintli canel titzontecon ca tiēlchīquiuh in ōmitzmonemactilì in tlācatl in totēcuiyo in iz cà in ichpōchtzīntli, ca yèhuatl īpan tinemiz ticte-

A trained speaker offers *congratulations to a married couple.*

Oh my youngest ones, you owe thanks to our Lord and to our Mother the holy church that governs us for tying you together and uniting you. Go conducting and leading yourselves calmly and prudently. Let the words of the Giver of life, his holy thing (sacrament) that He has made your property and inheritance, come to fruition. Exert all your effort (do your best to follow all the admonitions), my children. Serve your God and ruler. Beware lest you neglect yourselves; beware lest you follow the path of the rabbit, the deer; beware lest you fall from a precipice, lest you fall in the river.[8] You, the groom, since you are the head and trunk of the maiden here whom our Lord has given to you, are to busy yourself and work at what people need, water

quipanōz in tlein tētĕch monec in ātl in tlaqualli in tōnacăyōtl in tēchŏmiyōtia in tēchnăcăyōtia, àmo ticochtoz àmo tipāctoz, yè tīxtōçōz timotlacuitlahuīz in mocochiān in monecehuiāyān ticmàmattoz ticcochìtleuhtoz in mōmōztlae in tlein mochān mocalìtic tētĕch monec: canel yè inic màca çan tlamāmălli in ōtimāmăltilōc:

Auh in tèhuātl nochpōchtze ca çan yē nō ĭhui inic tonyez inic tocompializ in quiāhuatl in ithualli in tlācatl in totēcuiyo, ca aocmo in pīpĭlōtl in [f.2r] cōcŏnēyōtl ticmomacaz, ca yè huel īpan tīxtōçōz timotlacuitlahuīz in quēnin tichuīcaz ticòtlatoctiz in mocalìtic. Oc yōyohuaz timēhuaz tiquichpānaz ticàhuăchīz in īquiāhuac in ithual in tlācatl in totēcuiyo, niman yè in tētech monec in ātĕxātzintli in tlamātzoaltzintli: niman yè in mălăcătl in tzōtzopāztli inic tichuellamachtiz in moquich in ōmitzmonemactilì in tlācatl in totēcuiyo, canel yè inic ticihuātzīntli in mochān

and food, the sustenance that gives us bones and flesh. You are not to lie in sleep and pleasure; you are to be wakeful and take care of things in your resting place (your domicile). You are to be finding out and leaping from your bed to see what people in your house and home daily need, for it is not just any burden that has been put upon you.

And you, my daughter, you are to be the same way in guarding the household of our Lord. You are no longer to give yourself to childishness, for you are to be wakeful and take care of how you conduct and manage things in your house. When it is still dark you are to rise and sweep and sprinkle the entryway and patio of our Lord,[9] and then also (you are to see to) the food and drink that people need; and then also (you are to use) the spindle and the weaver's reed (or stick), so that you will please your husband whom our

in mocalìtic timotlacuitlahuīz titlàpiaz àmo titlanēmpolōz, ihuan timopiaz àmo tĕuhtli tlàçolli ticnemītiz, ca ye yèhuātlin inic titlaçòtlaloz timahuizçoaz. Ō, noxōcŏyōhuāne nopilhuāne, mā īxquich amotlàpaltzin xoconmochīhuilīcān, àço huel cemilhuitzintli amēchonmonemītilīz in tlācatl in totēcuiyo; ànocè ye iz huītz in ītĕtzin in īquăuhtzin, ca àmo toconmatì in quēnin mācuil màtlac ic tonnemì in ītlālticpactzinco. Ca çan īxquich centēntli cencamatl ic namechonnotlātlauhtilia, ic nocompachoa in amomātzin in amocxitzin, cŏcōliztli namēchonnocuītilīz, nictequipachōz in amīxtzin in amoyōllòtzin, noxōcŏyōhuane nopilhuāne: mā amēchmochicāhuilli in totēcuiyo Dios in īpalnemoaloni.

Auh ca nican ammonoltìtoquè in antēnānhuān, ōanquinmocnēlilìque in ītlachihualhuān in tlācatl in totēcuiyo in amocōzcāhuān in amoquetzalhuān: àço amocnōpiltiz àço amomàcēhualtiz inic yēctli

Lord has given to you, for as a woman, you are to take care of things, watch over things, and not let things go to ruin in your house and home; and keep yourself so that you do not live badly and in vice, for this is why you will be loved and honored. Oh my youngest ones, my children, exert all your effort. Perhaps our Lord will give you a long life, or perhaps His punishment will come, for we do not know how we will live in the future on His earth.[10] Only with these few words do I address you and kiss your hands and feet. I (do not wish to) make you ill (with long talking), I (do not wish to) disturb your spirits, my youngest ones, my children. May our Lord God the Giver of life grant you health.

The same speaker to the parents.

And you the mothers[11] who are here, the creatures of our Lord, your jewels and quetzal

qualli quinmòtlatoctilīz in īpalnemoāni: àço īntech azcēhuizquè, àço īntech ampàtizquè, àço ompōpōhuiz, àço onixtlāhuiz in amochōquiz in amotlaōcol in amēlcìcĭhuiliz: auh in amotlācazcaltil in amotlācahuapāhual àço yēctli qualli quinmoyōllōtilīz in ilhuicahuà in tlālticpaquè, àço īntech ozcēhuiz in amīx in amoyōllo, ihuan àço īntech tzĭcuēhuaz tlapāniz xōtlaz cuepōniz in ītlachīhualtzitzīnhuān in ītlayōcoxhuān in tlācatl in [f.2v] totēcuiyo inic oncan amonmottazquè amonmīximatizquè: mā yè xicmotēmachilīcan in tlōquè nāhuăque, ȳtechtzinco ximochixcāyĕcan, quēn conmonequiltiz in mōztla in huīptla. Ca çan īxquichtzin ic amīxpantzinco niquīça nitlăhuĭltēqui ic namechonnonepechtēquililia nictlātlauhtia in amīxtzin in amoy[ō]llòtzin, namēchonnotlapolōltiliz nopiltzīntzine cŏcŏliztli namēchonnocuītiliz.

plumes (your children) owe thanks to you: perhaps you will be so fortunate that the Giver of life will cause things to go well with them; perhaps through them you will be relieved and cured, perhaps your weeping, sorrow, and sighing will come to fruition,[12] and perhaps the Master of heaven and earth will inspire those whom you have brought up and raised to be good; perhaps through them you will have peace of mind, and creatures of our Lord will split and break off from them, will bloom and flower so that you will see and recognize yourselves in them.[13] Have confidence in the All-pervasive, be awaiting His future pleasure. That is all with which I awkwardly pass before you, I bow down to and address you. I (do not wish to) distract you (with further talk), my nobles, I (do not wish to) make you ill.

Tlācatle tlàtoānie notēlpōchtze nopiltzinzine cŏcŏliztli nimitzonnocuītilīz nictlapŏlōltīz in tēucyōtl in tlàtòcāyōtl: ca nican quimomàcēhuià quimocnōpilhuià in monānhuān in motàhuān in motēucyōtzin in motlàtòcāyōtzin: Cuix imicnōpil inmàcēhual, inic īmpampa timàāquiltìtihuītz, ītlà mitzmocxināmictilizquè, ōtiquinmocnēlilì: tlā quitīmalōcān tlā quimomàcēhuīcān in tēucyōtl in tlàtòcāyōtl in mahuiçōtl. Auh in iz cà in icnōquāuhtli in icnōōcēlōtl in āxcan ōconcuic in ōconmomàcēhui in īteōyōtzin in tlācatl in totēcuiyo inic quinmocētililia quinmocĕpănilhuia in tonāntzin Xantla yclexia; àço quitlaçòcāmatizquè, àço quimahuizmatizquè inic nīcān īmpampa ōtihuālmohuīcac in tiquinmomahuizçōtilīco in ticmonēxtilīco in motēucyōtzin in motlàtòcāyōtzin: ōtiquinmocnēlilì

The same speaker to the governor of the altepetl and after that to the members of the council.

Oh lord, oh ruler, oh my son,[14] oh my noble, I (do not wish to) make you ill, to distract your lordship and rulership. Your mothers and fathers (those present) here are enjoying your lordship and rulership. Are they so fortunate that you come entering here on their account and they detain you? They owe you thanks. Let them enjoy your lordship, rulership, and dignity. And as to the humble eagle-jaguar[15] (the man, or groom) here who today has taken and enjoyed the sacrament of our Lord by which our Mother the holy church unites and joins people, perhaps they will appreciate and honor the way you have come here on account of them, that you have come to honor them and manifest your lordship and rulership. Oh lord and ruler, your vassals—your fathers, mothers,

tlācatle tlàtoānie in momācēhualtzitzinhuān in mocnōnānhuān in mocnōtàhuān in motēchīuhcāhuān: cuix nel tiquinmotlànēhuilia, canel mocuitlapīlhuān ca màtlăpālhuān, ca tīmpōchŏuh ca tīmāhuēhuēuh, ca mocēhuăllōtitlantzīnco ca mècauhyōtitlantzīnco, ca mocuĕxāntzīnco ca momāmalhuăztzīnco catè tlācatle nopiltzīntzine. Auh ca nĭcān anmoyetzticatè in antotēucyōhuān in anquimocuitlahuià in ītcōca in īmāmălōca in ātl in tepētl in ōanquihuālmoyăcānilìtiàquè in tlācatl in totēlpōchtzin in tŏxhuĭuhtzin, ōanquimocnēlilìquè, auh ōanquimicnēlìquè in iz monoltìtoquè in tēnānhuān in tētàhuān in ōquinmocaquililì in [f.3r] tlācatl in totēcuiyo in inchōquiz in īntlaōcol, inic āxcan quitīmaloà quimomàcēhuià in īteōyōtzin inic ōquinmocētililì in tonāntzin Xanta yclexia in intlācazcaltil in intlācahuapahual in iz cà in ichpōchtzintli in conētzintli, auh in icnōquāuhtli in icnōōcēlōtl: tlā conmomàcēhuīcān tlā con-

and progenitors (aides)—owe you thanks. Are you indeed lending yourself to them for a time, since they are your vassals and you are the great tree in whose protective shadow and under whose governance they are, oh lord, oh my nobleman? And here are you, our lords, who care for the governance of the city (the council members), who have brought here the lord, our son, our grandchild (the governor); he owes you thanks, and so do the parents (of the bride and groom) present here whose weeping and sorrow our Lord has heard, so that today those whom they have brought up and raised, the young woman and child (the woman so recently a child herself) and the humble man (the eagle-jaguar), today enjoy His sacrament, by which our Mother the holy church has united them. Let them enjoy your beneficence and your parenthood. This is all

tīmalōcān in amotēicnēliltzin auh in amonānyōtzin in amotàyōtzin. Ca çan īxquichtzin ic namēchonnotlātlauhtilia, ic nicpachoa in amomātzin in amocxitzin notēlpōchtzitzinhuāne nopiltzīntzine.

Responde à este el Governador.

Ō, Papolòtze, ōticmotlacnēlilì, ōtiquimicnēlì in iz monoltìtoquè tēnānhuān, tētàhuān, auh in iz cà in icnōquāuhtli in icnōōcēlōtl, auh in tochpōch in āxcan ōquimomàcēhuìquè in īteōyōtzin in tlācatl in totēcuiyo, inic ōquinmocētililì nenāmictiliztica in tonāntzin Xanta yclexia: quēn quimonmonequilīlīz in tlōquè nāhuăquè in īpalnemoāni: tlā ītechtzinco tontochīxcāyecān, àço quinmochicāhuiliz, àço yēctli qualli quinmomaquilīz in īcāuhyōtzin àço quinmoyēcòtlatoctilīz in īpan in ītlayecoltilōcatzin, in măchè yèhuātl in necōni in elēhuilōni, inic oquinmocētililì inic ōquimomàcēhuìquè

with which I address you, with which I kiss your hands and feet, my sons, my nobles.

The governor replies to the latter,
the trained speaker.

Oh Pablo, all owe you thanks, the parents here owe you thanks, and the humble man here and our daughter, who have today enjoyed the sacrament of our Lord, by which our Mother the holy church has united them in matrimony. What will the All-pervasive, the Giver of life, desire for them? Let us be awaiting of Him whether He will give them health, whether He will give them a good portion of His time (a long life), whether He will guide them well in His service, which is especially to be desired, since He united them so that they have enjoyed holy matrimony. You have

in teōyōtica nenāmictiliztli. Ōtlacāuhqui in moyōllòtzin notēchiuhcāhue: tlā ximohuetzilti, tlā ximocēhui.

Responde otro principal al mesmo.

Ō, noxōcŏyōhue, ōticmocnēlilì in tlācatl in toxhuiuhtzin: auh ōtiquimicnēlì in iz monoltìtoquè in tēnānhuān in tētàhuān in tlācazcaltìquè in tlācahuapāuhquè, auh in tēhuānyōlquè in ōnĕltix in ōquinmocaquililì in tlācatl in totēcuiyo in īnchōquiz in īmēlcìcĭhuĭliz; auh in iz catè in totēlpōch in tochpōch in āxcan ōinmàcēhualtic in yteōyōtzin in tlācatl in totēcuiyo in ilhuicahuà in tlālticpaquè, auh in tonāntzin Xanta yclexia in tēchmotquilia in tēchmomāmālia, inic nenāmictiliztica ōquinmolpilì ōquinmocētililì [f.3v] auh ōtitēchicnēlì in timotĭăchcāhuān, ca nican ticcēpanmahuiçoà in īteōyotzin in tlācatl

spoken generously, my progenitor,[16] do take a seat and rest.

Another nobleman replies to the same.

Oh my youngest one, the lord our grandson (the governor) owes you thanks, and so do the parents present here, the raisers and educators of children, and the relatives, whose weeping and sighing have been realized and heard by our Lord. And our son and daughter here, who today have experienced the sacrament of our Lord the Master of heaven and earth and of our Mother the holy church, which governs us, so that it tied them and united them in matrimony (likewise owe you thanks). And we your elder brothers owe you thanks, for here we jointly honor the sacrament of our Lord, and we are enjoying the

in totēcuiyo, auh tictomàcēhuià in īntētlaçòtlaliz in iz monoltìtoquè tēnānhuān tētàhuān. Ōtimotlacnēlilì notēlpōchtze, tlā ximohuetzilti, tlā xicmocēhuili in monacayōtzin.

La madre del desposado al mesmo.

Noquichpiltzin noconētzin ōticmocnēlilì in tlācatl in tlàtoāni in totzontecon in techmotquilia in techmomāmālia in nican topampa màāquiltìtihuitz, cuix tocnōpil cuix tomàcēhual in tīcuitlapīlhuān in tiàtlăpălhuān in tictom̀àcēhuià in īteucyōtzin in ȳtlàtòcāyōtzin. Cuix nel techmotlànēhuilia? ca tīmācēhualhuān ca īcuĕxāntzīnco ca īmāmalhuāztzīnco ticatè, ca techmotquilia ca techmomāmālia. Auh ōtiquinmocnēlilì in totēcuiyōhuān in quimòtla[to]ctilià in ātl in tepētl: auh in iz catè in icnōtēlpōchtzīntli in icnōichpōchtzintli in impampa ic īxco titlachià in tāuh in totĕpēuh,

charity of the parents present here. All owe you thanks, my son. Do take a seat and give your body rest.

The mother of the groom to the same.

Oh my male child (my son),[17] the lord ruler, our head who governs us, who has come entering here on our account, owes you thanks. Are we his vassals so fortunate as to enjoy his lordship and rulership? Is he indeed lending himself to us for a while? We are his subjects and in his charge, for he governs us. And our lords who guide the city (the council members) owe you thanks, as do the humble young man and woman here on whose account we now face (the assembled) city,[18] because they have enjoyed the sacrament of our Lord the Giver of life, because our Mother the holy church

inic ōquimomàcēhuìquè in īteōyōtzin in tlācatl in totēcuiyo in īpalnemoāni. Auh inic oquinmocētililì nenāmictiliztica in tonāntzin Xanta yclexia, àço tocnōpil àço tomàcēhual mochīhuaz. Auh ca nō nicān ticcuì ticānà in mìhiyòtzin in motlàtōltzin in titēnānhuān in titētàhuān. auh in tēhuānyōlquè, ōtocnōpiltic ōtomàcēhualtic, tlā tictocuiltōnōcān tlā tictotlamachtīcan inic nican ōtēchmocēpantlālilì in tlācatl in totēcuiyo noquichpiltzin tlaçòtli tlācatzintli, yēctli oquichtzintli: mā ximocēhuìtzino, mā xicmocēhuili in monacayōtzin.

Mā ximēhuīltitiecān nopīltzintzĭne, namēchonnotlapololtilīz ca ye imman in. Quēn anconmomachītià in amonăcăyōtzin? Cuix tepitzin yēctli qualli ōāmēchmomàcēhualtilì in ītēchicāhualiztzin in tlācatl in totēcuiyo? Ca çan īxquichtzin inic nicnepechtēquilia in

has united them in matrimony. Perhaps it will become our good fortune. And here also we the parents profit from what you have said, and it has been the good fortune of the relatives (to hear it). Let us rejoice that our Lord has brought us together here. My male child, precious personage, proper man, do rest, put your body to rest.

Pablo's greeting to the company.

Do remain seated, my nobles. I (do not wish to) distract you. It's already late. How do you feel? Has our Lord given you the good fortune of a bit of His good health? That is all with which I bow down before your dignity and kiss your hands and feet.

amomahuizçōtzin, nicpachoa in amomātzin in amocxitzin.*

R[a.]

[f.4r] Ō, Papolotze otiquìīyōhuì, ōtitechicnēli: ca tel tepitzin tictomàcèhuià in ītēchicāhualiztzin in īpalnemoāni in nican ōtechmocēpanilhuīco. Quēnin? Quin ye imman in tiquīztihuitz tocnīuhtze? etts.†

* The word appears to read *anocxitzin,* but this has to be a copying error. A Spanish translation follows this paragraph, which is omitted here.

† A Spanish translation follows this paragraph as well.

Reply.

Greetings, Pablo. Thank you, yes, we are enjoying a bit of the health of the Giver of life, who has united us here. How then? Not until now do you come by, friend.

Lo que dicen los cihuàtlanques a los Pes. de la que es pedida del Rey de Tetzcuco.

Tlācatle, tlàtoānie nopiltzīntzine cihuāpille ticnepechtēquilià in tēucyōtl in tlàtòcāyōtl, ticpachoà in amomātzin in amocxitzin, ca nican amīxpantzinco ōtēchvalmihuālì in tlācatl in tlàtoāni .N.* in conmopachilhuia in ātl in tĕpētl in amochāntzīnco in Ācōlhuàcān Tetzcòco, ca quimìtalhuia: Tlā quimocaquītīcān in tlācatl in tlàtoāni in ātl ìtic onmotlàpielia in tochān in Mēxìco Tĕnŏchtitlan, īhuan in toquīzcān in toyōlcān in Ātzaqualco, in tlācatl .N. īhuan izcihuāpilli .N. canel yè inīc

* The writer is using a Spanish convention here: "N" for "Nombre," meaning in effect "insert name here."

PART II
The Past

What the bride-negotiators say to the parents of the bride requested by the King of Texcoco.

Oh lord, oh ruler, oh my nobleman, oh lady, we bow down to your lordship and rulership, we kiss your hands and feet, for the lord ruler [Name],[1] who governs the city, your[2] home, of Acolhuacan Texcoco, has sent us here before you, and he says: "Let the lord ruler within the waters,[3] who is in charge at our home of Mexico Tenochtitlan and in our place of origin of Atzacualco (the place of the dike, one of the subsections of Tenochtitlan), the lord [Name] and the lady [Name] listen, since that which forms the tuft and tassel of the tree of rulership

momălăcăyōtia momĭăhuăyōtia in Mīzquĭtl in Āhuēhuētl in Pōchōtl: ca ōmpa onhuetzi in nīx in noyōllo connequi conelēhuia ĭnīc mānŏço nomàcēhualti in īntlaçòchālchĭuh in īnteōxiuhtzin in īnmāquīz in ītozcatlantzīnco in īxĭllāntzīnco ōmopītz ōmomămăl in tlācātl izcihuāpilli in īnnecàcāhual in īnxōtlăca in īncuepōnca in tēteuctin in tlàtòquè in ōquimopĭĕlīcò in ātl in tĕpētl, auh in pĕtlătl in ĭcpălli in tochān in Mēxìco Tĕnŏchtītlan. Mā notech quihuālmotlālilīcān, mā ic nēchhuālmochìchīhuilīcān nēchhuālmonēxtilīcān, ca ye ōncān ca ye imman, canel àmo çan nicnotlànēhuilia canel nocozqui ca noquĕtzăl: auh intlā ītlà tomàcēhualtiz, intlā onyez īmàcēhual in ātl in tĕpētl, intlā huel quimocuīlīz intlā huel quimānĭlīz in tlōquè in nāhuăquè in ĭlhuĭcāhuà in tlāltĭcpăquè in tēyōcōyăni in tēchīhuăni in tochōquiz in totlaōcol ca tomàcēhualtiz cēmĕmè ōmĕmè in ītlăchīhualtzĭtzīnhuān in totech tzīcuēhuazquè in totech

has taken my heart.[4] I want and desire that I might enjoy their precious green stone, their fine turquoise, their bracelet that was forged and perforated at the throat and in the womb of the lady (i.e., their daughter), the relic and bloom of the lord rulers who have come to guard the city, (to occupy) the seat of authority in our home of Mexico Tenochtitlan. May they place her next to me, may they adorn her for me and show her to me, since the time has come, and I am not merely lending myself to her.[5] She is my jewel and quetzal plume. And if we are so fortunate, and the city is so fortunate, that the All-pervasive, the Master of heaven and earth, the Creator and engenderer of people, should hear our weeping and sorrow, we will be so fortunate that one or two of His creatures will split and break off from us, who will have their time in governing the city. When we have come to rest

tlăpānizquè, in yèhuān ceppătĭzquè in ītechpa in ītcōca in īmāmălōca in ātl in tĕpētl, in ōtozcēuhquè in ōtŏntlănquè, oc [f.4v] yèhuān īntech tōnaz īntech tlathuiz, canel yè inīc tŏncătè, cănĕl yè inīc tictotlàtōlchialilīcò in tlācatl in totēcuiyo in īlhuĭcăhuà tlāltĭcpăquè, mĭctlānè. Auh mā niman nŏcŏncăqui in īmìȳyōtzin in īntlàtōltzin inīquin onhuīlōaz in conmānilītihuì in tlācătl izcihuāpilli tohuēltīhuàtzin inīc conmopăchĭlhuīquīuh in īātzin in ītĕpētzin, auh in īpĕtlătzin in īcpăltzin, in ōncān ompōpōhuiz in ōncān ŏnĭxtlāhuiz inic nēchonmoyōllālilīz, ȳhuan inīc co[n]màcŏpăitztilìtiāzquè in īhuèpōltzitzīnhuān in īcihuāpòtzitzīnhuān, īhuan in īcuĭtlăpĭltzin in īàtlăpăltzin. Ō, totēcuiyōhuāne tlàtòquèe, ca yèhuatlin in anquimocaquītià in ìȳyōtzin in ītlàtōltzin in tlācătl in tlàtoāni amomăchtzin. Mā centēntli mā cĕncămătl ticcaquicān in amìȳyōtzin in amotlàtōltzin, inīc tictoyōllālilītīhuì in tlācatl in tlàtoāni, canel huālmochīxcāyetztzinòticà, canel iz

and to an end, there will be light through them, since that is why we exist, since that is why we have come to obey our Lord, the master of heaven, earth, and the underworld. Let me quickly hear word from them how a party will come to bring the lady, our elder sister,[6] to come to govern her city and occupy her throne, where it will come to fruition that she will console me, and her (little) brothers-in-law and sisters (in-law) and her vassals will be looking up to her." Oh our lords, oh rulers, these are the words of the lord ruler, your nephew,[7] that you hear. May we hear a few words from you with which we can go to console the lord ruler, since he is waiting, since it is here that his heart and eyes fall, oh our lords, oh rulers, oh lady, oh my lords.

huālhuetzticà in īxtzin in īyōllòtzin, totēcuiyōhuāne tlàtòquèe, tlācătle cihuāpille nopiltzīntzine.

Respuesta de los Padres de la moça.

Tlàtòquèe ōanquimìȳyōhuīltìquè in topampa anmàāquīltìtihuītzè ītlà tamēchtocxināmictilizquè, tēmōxtli èēcătl tamēchtocuītilīzquè: Cuix tocnōpil cuix tomàcēhual inīc topampa anmocĭănmĭctìtihuītzè in tĕpētl in ĭxtlāhuătl ōanquihuālmopănăhuilìquè: màcĭhui izçan nicān izçan ici in tochān in Tĕtzcòco Ācōlhuàcān, ca onāntĭcà. Auh ca ōtlacāuh in iyōllòtzin in tlācătl in tlàtoāni in tŏmăchtzin, ōtechmocnēlilì, auh ōquimocnēlilì in īmācēhuăltzin in īhuēltīhuàtzin in ichpŏcătzin tictotlănēhuià; cuix nel quimotlànēhuĭlia, ca iezço ca ȳtlăpăllo, māço ŏnyăuh ma conmotĕquĭpănīlhuì, mā onixtlāhui mā ompōpōhui inīc cihuātl īhuan inīc tētzon inīc tēĭzti, auh inic tētloc tēnāhuac ōmotlācătilì, cāmpa nel yāz, ca ye yèhuātl inīc

Reply of the parents of the girl.

Greetings, oh rulers who have come entering here on our account, we (do not wish to) detain you or bring illness upon you. Are we so fortunate that you have fatigued yourselves crossing hills and plains coming here on our account? Although our home of Texcoco Acolhuacan (is in the vicinity) it is a good stretch away. The lord ruler our nephew has spoken generously; we owe him thanks, and his vassal, the elder sister and humble girl, whom we have (with us) for a while, owes him thanks. Is he indeed lending himself to her? She is of his flesh and blood (his kin, his line). Let her go and serve him, let her be as she should be as a woman, as a person of high descent, born of important people. Where

ōquimochīhuilì inīc ōquimotlācătililì in ilhuicahuà in tlālticpaquè, canel ye ō ītech huetz in iīxtzin in iyōllòtzin in tlācatl in tlàtoāni tomăchtzin. Auh quēn conmonequiltiz in tlŏquè in nāhuaquè, àço huel cemilhuitzintli conmotēquīpānīlhuīz, auh conmotlàpielilīz in īquiyāhuactzīnco in īithualtzīnco in ōncān quimotlàtōlchiālīlīz: īhuan àço ītlà tolhuiltiz tomàcēhualtiz inīc cē [f.5r] ōmĕ icpac titlachiazque in ītlăchīhualhuān in tŏxhuīhuān in īntech tōnaz tlăthuĭz in īquin in cānin quimocēhuĭltīz in tlācatl in totēcuiyo, in cēmè yèhuān quimocācāxcēhuilīzquè quimoquĭmĭlcēhuilīzque, àço yèhuān cĕppātĭquīhuì tlătquĭquīhuì tlămāmāquīhuì. Auh inin tētēuctinè tlàtòquèe tlein nel tiquìtōzquè, mā yuh mochīhua mā yuh nĕlti in conmonĕquīltia in tlācatl in tlàtoāni tomăchtzin, ca iz onmoyetzticatè in mochtīntzitzin in tētēuctin in tlàtòquè Mēxìcà Tenochcà, ca izcĕpănĭāntlàtōltzin: auh ca ticchià in ìīyōtzin in ītlàtoltzin inīc onyāz in ĭcnōtlācăuhtzin

else should she go? This is why the Master of heaven and earth engendered her and caused her to be born, that she might take the eyes and heart of the lord ruler our nephew. What will be the will of the All-pervasive? Perhaps she will serve him for a lifetime and be in charge of his household, where she will do his bidding, and perhaps we will be so fortunate as to see one or two of his creatures, our grandchildren, through whom there will be light when our Lord gives him (the current ruler) rest, and one of them will relieve him of his burden and one day come to rule. Well, oh lords and rulers, what should we say then? Let it so be done, let what the lord ruler our nephew desires be realized: here are all the Mexica Tenochca lords and rulers, who jointly concur. We await word from him that his humble servant the maiden is to go. Take to your feet, oh rulers. Thus inform and consult

in ĭchpōchtzīntli: mā xoconmānilīcān in amocxitzin tlàtòquèe, mā yuh xoconmocăquĭztĭlĭlītin yuh xoconmonōnōchĭlītin in tlācatl in tlàtoāni tomachtzin: itlà tamechtocxināmictilīzquè, tictequipachōzquè in amīxtzin in amoyōllòtzin. Mā amoyōlīcàtzin totēcuiyōhuāne tlàtòquèe.

Saluda el desposado Rey à su esposa recien llegada.

Oticmìīyōhuiltì tlācatle cihuāpille, ca ōtimàxĭtīco in mochāntzīnco in oncān toconmotlàtōlchiālĭlīz in tlācatl in totēcuiyo in īlhuĭcāhuà in tlālticpaquè. Quēn conmonequiltīz, àço huel cĕmĭlhuitzīntli nimitzonnomàcēhuìtzinoz. Auh oanquimìīyōhuiltìquè tlàtòquèe cihuāpīpīltine namēchonnotlāxĭlīz ītlà namēchonnocxināmictilīz: mā ximocălăquīcān in amochāntzīnco.

with the lord ruler our nephew. We (do not wish to) detain you, to disturb your spirits. Take it easy then, oh our lords, oh rulers.

The king, now married, greets his recently arrived bride.

Greetings, oh lady, you have arrived at your home, where you will do the bidding of our Lord the Master of heaven and earth. What will be His will? Perhaps I will enjoy you for a whole lifetime. And greetings to you, oh rulers, oh ladies. I (do not wish to) inconvenience or detain you; do enter your home.

Un Principal de la Corte [del] Rey Saluda a la Reyna recien desposada.

Totēcuiyōe, cihuāpille, cihuātēuctzintle, tlăçòtzīntle, tlăçòtli tlācătle, tlaçòcōzcătle, chālchĭhuĭtle, māquīztle teōxĭhuĭtle, ōticmìīyōhuiltì, oticmocĭăhuīltì ca ōtimàxĭtīco in īpan in mātzin in motĕpētzin, in oncān ixtlāhuiz pōpōhuiz inīc toconmotequipanilhuīz in tlācatl tlàtoāni, ȳhuan in mohuèpōltzitzīnhuān in mohuĕzhuàtzĭtzīnhuan in mitzonmàcopaitztilìtiāzquè, īhuan in mocuĭtlăpĭltzin in màtlăpăltzin. Auh quēn conmonequiltīz in tlācatl in totēcuiyo in ĭlhuĭcăhuà in tlālticpăquè in mĭctlānè, àço tomàcēhualtiz tocnōpiltiz izcĕmĭlhuĭtzīntli timitzontocnōpilhuìtzinōzquè: īhuān àço çā nēn nō tocnōpiltiz inīc motechtzīnco tzīcuēhuaz tlăpāniz in tocōzqui in toquĕtzăl, àço xōtlaz àço cuĕpōniz in moxĭllāntzīnco in motŏzcătlantzinco in ĭtzmolĭnca in īcĕlĭca in īxōtlăca in tlācatl [f.5v] in tlàtoāni in tlācătēuctli,

A nobleman of the court of the king greets the recently married queen as a formal speaker.

Oh our mistress, oh noblewoman, oh lady, oh precious one, oh precious personage, oh precious jewel, oh green stone, oh bracelet, oh fine turquoise, many greetings. You have arrived in your city, where it will come to fruition that you will serve the lord ruler, and your brothers-in-law and your sisters-in-law and your vassals will be looking up to you. What will be the wish of our Lord the Master of heaven, earth, and the underworld? Perhaps we will be so fortunate as to have you for a lifetime, and I wonder if we will also be so fortunate that a jewel and quetzal plume of ours will split and break off from you, will bloom and blossom out from your womb and throat, the spout and blossom of the lord ruler, the Tlacateuctli.[8] Perhaps our Engenderer, the Master of the created, the Creator, the

àço çā huel cētzin ōmètzin quimomācāhuilīz quimochīhuiliz quimoyōcŏlĭlīz quimoyōlītĭliz quimŏzcălĭlīz in totēchīuhcātzin in tlachīhuălècātzintli in tlăyōcŏyăni in īpalnemoāni in tlācatl in totēcuiyo in teōtl in ītlāhuil in ītlănēx yĕtiuh in ātl in tĕpētl in oncān tōnaz in oncān tlathuiz, auh in quimocācāxcēhuilītiuh in quimoquĭmĭlcēhuilītīuh in tlācatl in tlàtoāni, in ìquāc in īquin quihuālmonōchilīz quihuālmotzàtzililīz in īpalnemoāni in tlŏquè nāhuăquè. Auh inin totēcuiyōe, cihuāpille, cŏcŏliztli ticmocuītīz: mā īxquich motlàpaltzin xoconmochīhuili, mā cemìcac xicmotēmachili xicmotlātlăuhtili in tlācatl in totēcuiyo xicmotlăōcōlnōnōchili inic mitzmocnēlilīz inīc mitzmomàcēhualtilīz: auh inīc īhuĭan yōcoxcā toconmotlàpiĕlĭlīz in īquĭāhuactzīnco in ĭthuăltzīnco: auh in ātl in tĕpētl in cuĭtlăpĭlli in àtlăpălli, inic mocēhuallōtitlantzinco mècauhyōtitlantzīnco calaquiz tlacnōpilhuīz. Ca çan īxquich ic mīxpan-

Giver of life, our divine Lord, will grant, engender, create, bring to life, and quicken one or two (children) who will be the illumination and splendor of the city, through whom there will be light, and who will relieve the lord ruler of his burden when the Giver of life, the All-pervasive, should summon and call to him. Well, oh our mistress, oh our lady, I (do not wish to) bring you illness (through long talk). Exert every effort. Always have confidence in our Lord and pray to Him; call for His mercy, to benefit you and make you deserving, and that you gently and prudently watch over His household, and that the city and the commoners be so fortunate as to enter into your protective shade. This is all with which I appear before you and bow down to your ladyship and womanly rulership, with which I kiss your hands and feet, with which I bow down to you and with which your city

tzinco ninēci nicnepechtēquilia in motēucyōtzin in mocihuāpillàtòcāyōtzin, ic nicpachoa in momātzin in mocxitzin, ic nimitznonepechtēquililia, īhuan in mātzin motĕpētzin ic mitzmonepechtēquililia, ic mitzmotlātlăuhtilia, ca nicān mīxpantzīnco nictlàtalhuia nictlătēnquīxtilia, tlăcătle cihuāpille nopīltzīntzine.

El mesmo habla al Rey desposado.

Totēcuiyōe, tlācatle, tlàtoānie, xōcŏyōtle, tlaçòtle, māquīztle, tēoxihuitle chālchĭhuĭtle, quĕtzăle, ātle, tĕpētle, ca ōtocnōpiltic, ca ōtomàcēhualtic inic ōtocmŏlpĭlìtzinò in tlaçòmāquīztetl, in motŏzcătlāntzīnco ōtoconmotlālilì in tlaçòchayāhuaccōzcătl: auh in mocpac ōtoconmoquĕchĭlì in quĕtzălli pătlāhuac in ōtoconmonĕpănĭlhuì in tēcpīllōtl in măhuĭzçōtl in àcōpăitztoz, in ītech onhuetztoz in ix in īyōllo in mātzin in motĕpētzin, auh in mocuĭtlăpĭltzin in

bows down to you and addresses you, for I speak for the city here before you, oh lady, oh my noble person.

The same man speaks to the married king.

Oh our lord, oh personage, oh ruler, oh youngest one, oh precious one, oh bracelet, fine turquoise, green stone, quetzal plume, oh ruler of the city, we have been so fortunate that you have tied on the precious bracelet, have placed at your throat the precious necklace with radiating pendants, and on your head you have raised the wide quetzal plumes; you have brought together the nobility and dignity to which your city looks up and of which it is enamored, and which your

màtlăpăltzin in ītech motēmachìtiez mochīxcāyez. Mā ic cencà mohuellamachti, mā ic mocuiltōno in ītēicnēliltzin in tlācatl in totēcuiyo in īpalnemoāni. Quēn conmonequīltīz in mōztla in huĭptla in mācuil in màtlac: mā titochīxcāyĕcān inic àço tomàcēhualtiz, àço xōtlaz àço cuĕpōniz cē ōmĕ in ītlăchīhualtzitzinhuān totēcuiyo in īpalnemoāni, àço mopītzaz àço momămălīz in tlaçòchālchĭhuitl teōxĭhuĭtl in āqu[in] mitzonmocācāxpătilīz, mitzonmoquĭmīlpătilīz in ītech tōnaz in ītech tlăthuĭz, in īquin mitzhuālmonōchilīz in īquin mitzhuālmā[f.6r]nīlīz in ilhuĭcāhuà in tlāltĭcpăquè. Tlā tocontīmalōcān tlā toconmàcēhuăcān in āxcan quitta in āxcan quimahuiçoa in mātzin in motĕpētzin, tlācătle tlàtoānie. Ca çan īxquĭch tzŏcōtzin ic timitztonepechtēquililià ic ticpachoà in momātzin in mocxitzin tlācatle totēcuiyōe.

vassals will be expecting and awaiting. Rejoice greatly in the beneficence of our Lord the Giver of life. What will be His will in the future? Let us be hoping that perhaps we will be so fortunate that one or two of the creatures of our Lord the Giver of life will bloom and flower. Perhaps there will be forged and perforated the precious green stone and fine turquoise who will take up your burden and through whom there will be light when the Master of heaven and earth summons and takes you. Let us enjoy what our city today is seeing and beholding, oh lord, oh ruler. This is everything with which I bow down to you and kiss your hands and feet, oh lord, our lord.

Salutacion a la Reyna parida.

Totēcuiyōe cihuāpille, chālchĭhuĭtle cōzcătle teōxĭhuĭtle māquīztle, tlā īxquich motlàpaltzin: ca ye ōquimonequiltì in tlācatl in totēcuiyo in ilhuicahuà in tlāltĭcpăquè, ca ye ōquimottilì ca ye ōquimocaquītì in īchōquiz in ītlăōcol in mātzin in motĕpētzin, ca ye ōmopītz, ca ye ōmomămăl in tlaçòmāquīztētl in tlaçòchālchĭhuĭtl, ca ye ōtomàcēhualtic ca ye ōtocnōpiltic in oquichtzintli ōmotlācătĭlì; àço īmàcēhual yez in ātl in tĕpētl, intlā mozcaltīz intlā mohuăpāhuaz, ca imàcēhual yez in cuitlăpĭlli. quēnămì ic ōquimonăhuătĭlì in tlŏquè nāhuăquè in ĭlhuĭcăhuà in mĭctlānè: ma ticmoxiccāhuilì in īca in īchīchīhuăltzin, īpan timotlàtōltīz inīc conmocuitlahuīzquè in māhuītzĭtzīnhuān in mocìhuān. Mā ixquich motlàpaltzin xoconmochīhuili totēcuiyōe cihuāpille, cocoliztli ticmocuītiz, tequipachihuiz in mīxtzin

The trained speaker offers *salutation to the queen after she has given birth.*

Oh our mistress, oh lady, oh green stone, oh jewel, oh turquoise, oh bracelet, be of good cheer, for now it has been the will of our Lord the Master of heaven and earth that He has seen and heard the weeping and sorrow of your city, and the precious bracelet, the precious green stone has been forged and perforated, and we have been so fortunate that a boy has been born. Perhaps if he grows up he will become the fortune of the city, of the commoners. As the All-pervasive, the Master of heaven and the underworld dispatched him, do not neglect his breastfeeding, see to it that your attendants care for him. Exert every effort (taking care of the boy), oh our mistress, oh lady. I (do not wish) you to take ill or for your spirit to be disturbed. May you profit

in moyōllòtzin. Mā īhuiān xoconmocuīli xoconmānili in tlamātzŏhuăltzintli, tlācatle cihuāpille nopiltzīntzĭne.

Parabien al Rey del niño nacido.

Tlācătle totēcuiyōe, tlàtoānie tlaçòtzīntle tlaçòtli tlācătle ōīmàcēhualtic in mātzin in motĕpētzin in cuĭtlăpilli in àtlăpălli: auh ōtomàcēhualtic ōtocnōpiltic inīc āxcan ōticmottilì in tlaçòchālchĭhuĭtl in tēōxĭhuĭtl in motechtzīnco ōtzīcuēuh in motechtzīnco ōtlăpan in ōmitzmomaquilì in tlācatl in totēcuiyo in ĭlhuĭcăhuà in tlāltĭcpăquè in tēchīhuăni in tēyōcōyăni in ōmitz[m]omaquili in ōmitzhuālmihuālilì in tlaçòchālchĭhuĭtl in tēōxĭhuĭtl in māquīztētl in āxcan ticmocōzcătìtzinoa ticmomàcuĕxtìtzīnoa: Mā conmahuiço, mā contīmalo in mātzin in motĕpētzin: mā ic onmohuellamachti. Ōtomàcēhualtic tlācătle totēcuiyōe tlàtoānie.

from your diet, oh personage, oh lady, oh my noblewoman.

Congratulations to the king on the birth of the child.

Oh personage, oh lord, oh our ruler, oh precious one, oh precious personage, your city and the commoners have been fortunate; we have been so fortunate that today you have seen the precious green stone, the fine turquoise, that has split and broken off from you, that our Lord the master of heaven and earth, the Engenderer and Creator of people, has given you. May your city behold, enjoy and rejoice in the precious green stone, the fine turquoise, the bracelet that He has given and sent you and that you now take as your necklace and bracelet. We have been fortunate, oh personage, oh our lord, oh ruler.

Saludan al Rey muerto.

Tlācătle tlàtoānie ca ye ōtimotēquĭltilì, ca ye ōtimotlācòtilì, ca ye ōompōpōuh ca ye onixtlāuh in itcōca in īmāmālōca in mātzin in motĕ-[f.6v] pētzin, inic mocuĕxāntzīnco momāmălhuāztzīnco ōcatca, ca àmo īhuĭān yōcoxcā inic ōticmonāpălhuīco, inīc ōticmomāmālīco in mātzin in motĕpētzin, ca huel onquīz, ca huel ontlàtlan in tōnēhuiztli in chĭchĭnaquiztli in īpampa ōticmìīyōhuiltīco ōticmocĭăhuīltico, ca īhuiān ca yōcoxcā in ōticmotlālcāhuilì in mātzin in motĕpētzin, ca īhuiān ca yōcoxcā in ōtonmohuētzītīco in petlapan in icpalpan, ca tlămăch in ōtoconmotlătlàtlālilico in toconmotlatètēquililīco in īpalnemoāni. Auh ca nēllĭ măch in ontlàtlămico in mìīyōtzin, nēlli mach in ō īpan tihuālmòōnōltìtià in ātl in tepētl. Otimoçòçouhtzinōco in īxpantzīnco totēcuiyo, àmo momātzin àmo mocxitzin ō motlantzīnco ticmāquilīco. Auh

Salute to the dead king.

Oh personage, oh ruler, you have already worked and served, and the governance of your city, while it was in your charge, was as it should be, for it was not quietly and gently (but with much effort) that you governed your city. The suffering and pain from tiring and fatiguing yourself have come fully to an end and a conclusion; you have left your city in peace, (as) in peace you came to occupy the mat and seat of authority. Peacefully you arranged and settled things for the Giver of life. Truly indeed you spent all your breath, truly indeed you exerted yourself on behalf of the city. You stretched yourself out (were active) before our Lord. You did not idly hide your hands and feet under your cape. And now there is silence and darkness in your city. Your vassals are wrapped in weeping and sorrow, as are the nobles whom you have

in āxcā ca ye căctimani, ca ye yŏhuătimani in īpan in mātzin in motĕpētzin: auh chōquiztli tlăōcŏlli ic mĭlăcătzòtoc in mocuĭtlăpĭltzin in màtlăpăltzin, auh in tēpilhuān ōtiquinmocnōcāhuilìtēhuac, çā īnēncāuhyān quimochīhuilia in tlācatl in totēcuiyo. À ōtiquimonmomachīti, à ōtiquimonmotŏquĭlì. à īntech ōtimàxitīto in măchcòcōlhuān in motēchīuhcāhuan? ca otoconmotŏquĭli, ca ītech ōtimàxītì in tonān in totâ: in màca çan cănà huīloa, mach oc tihuālmīlōchtīz? mach oc tihuālmocuēptzinoz? cuix oc mācuil, cuix oc màtlac mitzmochiālīz in māuh in motĕpēuh? auh in mozte in motzon? ca niman aocmo: ca ye īxquich ca ye yuhqui, ca ye ō ȳcĕnmănyān timohuīcac, ca ye ōpŏlĭuh ca ye ōcēuh in ŏcŏtl in tlāhuĭlli, ca ye căctĭmăni ca ye yŏhuătimăni in iātzin in ītĕpētzin in tlŏquè in nāhuăquè. Mā onchōca, mā ontlăōcŏya in cuĭtlăpĭlli in àtlăpălli, auh in tētzon in tēizti, in tēpilhuān, mā ompīpĭxăhui mā ontētĕpēhui

left orphaned; our Lord has made it a desolate place. Have you not gone to and reached your forebears and progenitors? You have gone to and reached our mother, our father. From the place where people go, not just anywhere, will you ever come back again? Will you return? Are your city and your offspring to expect you in the future? No, never again. For that is all, that is enough. You have gone once and for all. The torch and light have gone out and been snuffed. The city of the All-pervasive lies silent and dark. Let the commoners weep and sorrow, and let the tears of the wellborn, the nobles, sprinkle and scatter down. Let them cry in sorrow to the Giver of life, the All-pervasive; let them say, "Alas, woe to us who have been left orphans." Let there be weeping, sorrowing, and sighing; let the tears sprinkle and scatter down. Rest, rejoice next to your grandfathers and forebears whom you have

in īmīxāyo: Mā conmotlăōcōlnōnōchĭli in īpalnemoāni in tlŏquè in nāhuăquè, mā quìto in iyoyahue ōtotlahueliltic in ōticnōcāhuălōtēhuăquè. Tla chōcoa, tlā tlăōcŏyălo, tlā onelcìciyohua, tlā ompīpĭxăhui tlā ontētĕpēhui in īxāyōtl. Auh tlā ximocēhuìtzīno, tlā ximotlamachtìtzīno in innāhuac in măchtōnhuān in mocòcōlhuān in ōtiquimonmotŏquilì ō nō īntech tonmàxìtì in cānin xīmōhuăyān in tocenchān. Ca çan īxquich ic nimitznotlàpalhuia inic nimitznonepechtēquililia, ic tēīxtlan nonquīça totēcuiyōe, tlăcătle tlàtoānie. [f.7r]

El mesmo da el pesame de la muerte del Rey a los Principales.

Totēcuiyōhuāne, tlàtòquèe, pīpiltine, āhuàquèe, tĕpēhuàquèe, anca nēlli āxcan ōyà ōmotēcăto in tlăcătl .N. in ōquimopŏlhuì in ōquimotlātilì in totēcuiyo in ĭlhuĭcăhuà in tlālticpăquè in mĭctlānê;

gone to and reached in the fleshless place, our eternal home.[9] This is all with which I greet you and bow down to you, with which I appear before the public, oh lord ruler.

The same speaker gives condolences to the noblemen on the death of the king.

Oh our lords, oh rulers, oh nobles, oh citizens, thus today the lord [Name] whom our Lord the Master of heaven, earth, and the underworld has effaced and sequestered, has gone to rest. He has

Ōconquetztēhuac ōconcauhtēhuac in quĭmĭlli in cācāxtli in tlătcōni in tlămāmălōni in ĕtic in àēhualiztli in àīxnāmiquiliztli: à mach oc quihuālmati in īāuh in ītĕpēuh in căctĭmăni in ye yŏhuătĭmăni, in ye inēncāuhyān quimochīhuilia in tlŏquè in nāhuăquè. à mach oc huāllamati in ye cĕnquăhuĭtl ye cĕmĭxtlāhuătl măntiuh in tlătquitl in tlămāmalli in ōicnōcāhualōc in ōquicnōcāuhtēhuac in tlācatl in tlàtoāni in tlācatēuctli in nicān mēhuitìticà in ticchōquilià in ītlāllo in īçoquiyo, in ō cuēl ăchīc in ō ăchìtōnca quimotlănēhuì in ātl in tĕpētl in ōquitēmic in ōquicochìtlēuh, ca ōquihuālmonōchilì ca ōquihuālmotzàtzililì in tlācatl in totēcuiyo. Auh in tlālli izçŏquĭtl mā imānāhual, mā īquĕchtĕtzon mochīuhto in ātl in tĕpētl. Auh ca ye quimotōptēmilia ca ye quimopetlācaltēmilia in tlŏquè in nāhuăquè. à ōquimonmà à ōquimontŏcac? auh ca ō īntech onàcic in īăchcòcōlhuān in ītēchīuhcāhuān, ca ōcontŏcac ca ō ītech onàcic in tonān in totà,

put aside and left the bundle and carrying frame, the means of bearing the heavy, unliftable, unbearable load of government. Does he not still haunt his city, which lies in silence and darkness, which the All-pervasive has made a place of desolation? Does he not still haunt what now is an entirely deserted place, the governorship that the lord ruler, the Tlacateuctli, abandoned and orphaned, he who presided here, he over whose body we weep, who for a short time the city borrowed, dreamed, and saw in its sleep, for our Lord has summoned and called to him. Let the city provide safekeeping for his body. The All-pervasive has already put him in a chest, a reed basket. Has he not gone to and reached our mother, our father? He has gone to our eternal home, the place without a chimney, for he has already extinguished (the flame). He has gone to the place without fleas, the place where people

ca ontlamà in tocenchān in àpōchquiāhuăyòcān in àtlĕcăllòcān, ca ye quicēhuìtoc, ca ontlamà in mìtoa in àtĕcpĭntlà in màcă çan cănà huīloa, mach oc huālīlōtiz? mach oc huālmocuĕpaz? ca ye īxquich, ca ye yuhqui, ca ōcenonquīz ca ō cenmănyān catca, ca centlamic quimati in ātl in tĕpētl, ca aocmo mācuil màtlac onquīçăquiuh onmoquetzaquiuh: auh ca ōyà ca ōpŏliuh, ca ōcēuh in ŏcŏtl in tlāhuĭlli, ca ye cactimani ca ye yŏhuătimani in iātzin in ītepētzin tlŏquè nāhuăquè in īpalnemŏălōni. Anca oncanin ōconcāuhtēhuac ōconquetztēhuac in quĭmĭlli in cācāxtli in tlătcōni in tlamāmălōni, ca īhuiān yōcōxcā in ōquimotlālcāhuilì in ātl in tĕpētl, ca īhuian yōcōxcā in ōyeco in pĕtlăpan in ĭcpălpan, ca tlămăch ōcontlătlàtlālīlīco ōcontlătètēquililīco in īpalnemoāni. Auh ca nēlli mach in ōontlàtlămico in ìīyo nēlli mach in īpan ōhuālòōnŏtià in ātl in tĕpētl, ōmoçòçōhuăco in īxpantzīnco in tlācatl in totēcuiyo: àmo īma àmo icxi ō ītlan càaquīco, ca

go that is not just anywhere.[10] Will he ever come back again? Will he yet return? [No.] It is over, it is enough, it has ended once and for all. It was forever, and the city knows it is entirely finished, and he will not emerge and rise in the future. He has gone, he has disappeared. The torch and light have been snuffed out. The city of the All-pervasive and Giver of life lies silent and dark. So that here at this time he has relinquished and put up the bundle and carrying frame, the means of government. In peace he has abandoned the city, as in peace he occupied the mat and seat of authority, and peacefully he arranged and settled things for the Giver of life. Truly he expended all his breath. Truly he exerted himself on behalf of the city. He stretched himself out (was active) before our Lord. He did not idly hide his hands and feet under his cape. He exerted all his effort; his spirit suffered. Not quietly and gently (but

īxquich itlàpal ōquimochīhuilì, ca ōontòtōnēhuăco in īx in iyōllo [f.7v] ca àmo īhuiān ca àmo yōcōxcā in ōyĕco in īpĕtlăpan in īcpălpan in tlŏquè in nāhuăquè, ca àmo īcŏchīz ca àmo ītlăquăl ōquihuālmătĭco, ca ō īpampa tōnēhuăco in ātl in tĕpētl, ōīxtōçōco ōmocochìçōlōco in onelcìcĭhuico in ōonchōcăco, in ō īca in ō īpampa màmănăco in cuĭtlăpĭlli in àtlăpălli inīc onyĕco in īpĕtlăpan in īcpălpan in tlācătl in totēcuiyo. Auh inīc ōcŏnĭtquĭco inīc ōconmāmāco in ātl in tepētl. Ō, totēcuiyōhuāne tlàtòquèe, pīpīltĭne āhuàquèe, tĕpēhuàquèe, tlā īxquich amotlàpaltzin, tlā ontīmalihui, tlā onnetlămăchtĭlo in chōquiztli in tlăōcōlli, auh in īxāyōtl in elcìcĭhuĭlĭztli: ca çan īxquich ic amīxtlàtzinco niquīça, namēchonnonepechtēquilia niquēllaquāhua in amīxtzin in amoyōllòtzin. Tlā īxquich amotlàpaltzin, cŏcōliztli namēchonnocuītiliz totēcuiyōhuāne, tlàtòquèe, nopiltzīntzine.

by dint of great effort) did he sit on the throne of the All-pervasive. He knew no sleep, and no food (in difficult times). He suffered on account of the city; he kept vigil and went without sleep. He sighed and wept; he disquieted himself over the commoners when he was on the throne of our Lord and governed the city.[11] Oh our lords, oh rulers, oh nobles, oh citizens, make every effort. Let the weeping, sorrow, tears, and sighs increase and flourish. This is all with which I appear before you, bow down to you, and encourage your spirits. Be of good cheer. I (do not wish to) cause you to take ill (with long talking). Oh our lords, oh rulers, oh noblemen.

Avisos de buena criança a unos niños de un viejo.

Tlā tihuiān in īchāntzīnco in totēcuiyo, titlătlātlăuhtītīhuì ticcăquĭtīhuì in īteōyōtzin. Nīxpan ximăntĭhuĭān, àmo ximotōtŏpēuhtihuiān, xiyēcmăntĭhuĭan, àmo xìīxtlăpălitztihuian xiīxtŏmahuătihuiān. Quìtōzquè àço amotech quĭnēhua. Auh intlā cănà antēnāmĭquĭzquè, xitētlàpălōcān xitēnōtzăcān. Auh intlā cēmè yèhuāntzĭtzin pīpīltin, nocè in tētēuctin amotēchīuhcāhuān in quitquì quimāmà āltĕpētl, nŏcè huēhuetquè ĭlămătquè, oc chĭcŏtlănāhuac anmoquetzazquè in ŏquīc quīztihuì, anquinnepechtēquilià: mānēn antētŏpēuhtin ăntētlāztin.

PART III
Return to the Present

Advice on good breeding from an old man[1] *to some boys.*

Let us go to the house of our Lord to pray and hear His holy offices. Go along spread out in front of me, don't go shoving each other. Go along properly, don't go looking sideways and making faces. People will say that with you the shot missed. And if you meet someone somewhere, greet the person and speak to him. If it is one of the nobles, or one of the lords your progenitors who rule the city, or an old man or an old woman, you are to stand to one side until they pass by, and bow down to them. Don't shove anyone or knock them down.

Xiccaquicān noxōcŏyōhuāne ca àmo qualli in miec cŏchĭztli, ca cŏcōliztli īhuan tlatzĭhuĭztli quitēcuītia: oc yōyohuac ximēhuacān ic ampāctinemizquè, àmo ametīxtinemizquè. Cuix àmo no yuh ōmŏzcăltìquè in tlàtòquè amechmocāhuilìtihui? Cānmach mìtò in huel ōniquimiztlācò in huel ōniquimittac.

Saluda un muchacho noble a un religioso.

Nicnepechtēquilia in moteōpīxcāyōtzīn notlaçòtàtzine, nictēnnāmiqui in moteōpixcāmātzin, nictequipachōz in mīxtzin in moyōllòtzin, mēlchĭquĭuhtzin niquēhuaz. Quēn ticmomachīltia in moteōpixcānăcăyōtzin? cuix ticmomàcēhuìtzīnoa in ītēchicāhualiztzin in totēcuiyo in ĭlhuĭcăhuà in tlāltĭcpăquè? cuix nŏcè ītlà mopantzīnco quihuālmihuā- [f.8r] lia in ītēmōxtzin in īèēcătzin?

Listen, my youngest ones, much sleeping is bad, for it makes people fall ill and grow idle. Get up early in the morning, and that way you will live in health and not be heavy with sickness. Were not the rulers who left you behind (who came before you) brought up the same way? How is it that it was said that I really spied and saw these things?! (In other words, I am old and I know what I am talking about!)

A noble boy greets a friar.

I bow down to your priestliness, my precious father. I kiss your priestly hands; I (do not wish to) disturb your spirit or cause you stomach pains (with my importuning). What is the state of your priestly body? Are you enjoying the health of our Lord the Master of heaven and earth? Or has he sent upon you some of His afflictions?

R[a.]

Ōtinēchicnēlì, ca tepitzin oc cĕmīlhuĭtzīntli noconnomàcēhuia in ītēchicāhualiztzin in totēcuiyo: auh in tèhuātl quēn ticà: ȳhuan izcihuāpilli mocìtzin, īhuan izcihuāpilli monāntzin quēn moyetzticate? cuix quinmochicāhuilia in totēcuiyo?

Ōtiquinmocnēlilì notlăçòtàtzine, ca achìtzin quinmochicāhuilia in totēcuiyo. Çan ye nō ihui in nèhuātl nimŏcnōmācēhuăltzin ca nō tĕpĭtzin nicnomàcēhuia in īcĕmīlhuĭtzin in īpalnemoāni.

Saludan dos muchachos nobles à su aguela.

Notēcuiyōe tlācatle cihuāpille, cocoliztli timitztocuītilīzquè timitztotlăpŏlōltīlīzquè, ca ye īnmăn īn, àço achìtzin yēctli qualli ic ōmitzmotlăthuīltilì in totēcuiyo, àço tepitzin ticmomàcēhuìtzinoa in ītēchcāhualiztzin.

Reply.

Thank you. For another day I am enjoying a bit of the health of our Lord. And how are you? And how is your lady grandmother and your lady mother? Is the Lord giving them health?

Reply.

Thank you, my precious father. Our Lord is giving them a bit of His health. And likewise, I your humble vassal also am enjoying a little the day of the Giver of life.

Two noble boys greet their grandmother.

Oh our mistress, oh personage, oh lady, we (do not wish to) cause you illness or distract you, for it is late. Perhaps our Lord has caused you to rise feeling somewhat well. Perhaps you are enjoying a bit of His good health?

Responde ella brevamente; y luego habla con su ayo.

Ōanquìīyōhuìquè xōlōtōn: xicălăquĭcān. xiquinmocalaquili notēchīuhcāuh: mā ītlà conìtlacòtin: mitzmotolīnilià in moxhuīhuān.

Habla con ellos un Principal.

Tlā iz anmohuīcatze noxōcŏyōhuāne noxhuīhuāne. Intlā oc amīxco amocpac tlachianì in tētēuctin in tlàtòquè amotēchīuhcāhuān, quēnin cencà motlaçòcāmatizquià amēchmochōquilizquià? ca amītzŏnhuān ca amīxtĕhuān* in tlācatl in tlàtoāni in huēy tiàcāuh: auh ca amincōzqui ca aminquĕtzăl in tlācatl in tlàtoāni Ācătlmāpīchtli†

* The "x" here should be "z."

† The writer intends "Acamapichtli." He rightly realizes that "Acatl" is the embedded descriptor and for some reason writes it in full.

She replies briefly and then speaks to their tutor.

Greetings, little pages, come in. Bring them in, my progenitor.[2] Let them not damage anything. Your grandchildren (your charges) cause you too much trouble.

A nobleman speaks to them.

Do come here, my youngest ones, my grandchildren. If the lords and rulers your progenitors were to behold you, how very grateful they would be, and how they would cry over you! For you are the offspring of the lord ruler, the great leader, and you are descended from the lord Acamapichtli Nezahualpilli and the lord Acolmiztli Nezahualcoyotl, who stands (farther back in time). What will be the will of our Lord, the All-pervasive? Perhaps he will raise and bring you up. Perhaps we your mothers and fathers,

Nĕçăhuălpĭlli: auh in ye nechca mìcatiltìtĭuh in tlācatl in Ācōlmiztli Nĕçăhuălcŏyōtl. Quēn quimonequiltiz in tlācatl in totēcuiyo, tlŏquè nāhuăquè? àço amēchmŏzcăltīlīz ăço amēchmohuăpāhuilīz, àço huel cĕmĭlhuĭtzīntli amēchmomàcēhuīzquè in amonānhuān in amotàhuān in āhuàquè in tĕpēhuàquè. Mā tlăcāhua in īyōllòtzin mā tocēpanmàcēhualti. Mā xiquinmomàcēhuìtzīno tlācătle, cĭhuāpĭlle in ītlachīhualtzitzīnhuān in tlācătl in totēcuiyo in innecāuhcāhuān in tētēuctin in tlàtòquè māchcòcōltzitzīnhuān motēchīuhcāhuān. Tlā ximocalaquìtihuiān noxhuĭuhtzitzīnhuāne.*

Respondele por ellos su ayo.

[f.8v] Totēcuiyōe tlàtoānie ōtiquinmocnelilì in moxhuiuhtzitzīnhuān tēmōxtli èēcatl cŏcōliztli

* There is a rare mistake here: the original has a second breve diacritic over the "uh" intended to signify "w." Something similar occurs one more time in the document.

the citizens, will enjoy you for a lifetime. May He grant it. May we all be so fortunate. May you, oh personage, oh lady, enjoy the creatures of our Lord, as left to us by the lords and rulers, your forebears and progenitors. Do come in, my grandchildren.

Their tutor answers for them.

Oh our lord, oh ruler, your grandchildren owe you thanks. They (do not wish to) cause you illness or stomach pains or give you sorrow; here they profit from and enjoy your lordship and

mitzmocuītilīzquè mēlchiquiuhtzin conēhuazquè mitzmotlaōcolmăquĭlīzquè; ca nicān quicuì ca nicān cānà quimomàcēhuià in motēucyōtzin in motlàtòcāyōtzin, ōimicnōpiltic ōinmàcēhualtic in mìīyōtzin in motlàtōltzin. Xicălăquicān nŏxhuīhuāne.

Saluda el hijo mayor à su madre.

Notēcuiyōe cihuāpille nictēnnāmiqui in momātzin in moxcitzin, nicnepechtēquilia in momahuizçōtzin. Quēn ōmitzmotlathuiltilì in tlācatl in totēcuiyo? Cuix achìtzin ticmomàcēhuìtzinoa in ītēchicāhualiztzin?

A la mesma saluda el hijo menor.

Nopiltzīntzine, tlācatle, cihuāpille timitztotlapŏlōltilīzquè, timitztonepechtēquililià, tictlàpaloà in tēucyōtl in tlàtòcāyōtl: quēn ōticmomàcēhuìtzinò in cochiztli, auh in āxcan in

rulership, they have been fortunate to hear your words. Come in, my grandchildren.

The older son greets his mother.

Oh our mistress, oh lady, I kiss your hands and feet, I bow down to your dignity. How did our Lord cause you to feel on rising? Do you enjoy a bit of His health?

The younger son greets the same.

Oh my noble person, oh personage, oh lady, we (do not wish to) distract you; we bow down to you, we salute your ladyship and rulership. How did you enjoy your sleep, and now how

tlàcàtli? cuix tĕpĭtzin yēctli quălli ticmotīmalhuia ticmomàcēhuìtzinoa in ītēchicāhualiztzin in tlŏquè nāhuăquè in īpalnemōāni?

Responde la madre brevemente.

Ōanquìīyōhuìquè xōlōtŏtōn. Xicmotlàpalhuīcān in tlācatl amotēchīuhcāuh.

Saludan ambos muchachos à una principala anciana

Tlācătle, cihuāpille timitztotlapŏlōltĭlīzquè cocoliztli timitztocuītilizquè mēlchĭquĭuhtzin tiquēhuazque. Quēn ticmomăchīltia in monăcăyōtzin? cuix achìtzin ticmomàcēhuìtzinò in ītēchicāhualiztzin in tlācatl in totēcuiyo? Cuix nocè ītlà mopantzinco huālēhuaznequi in ītĕtzin in īquăuhtzin? Mā īxquich motlàpăltzin xoconmochīhuili nopiltzīntzine tlācătle, cihuāpille.

are you enjoying the day? Are you enjoying a bit of the good health of the All-pervasive, the Giver of life?

The mother briefly replies.

Greetings, little pages. Greet the lady your progenitor.

Both boys greet an elderly noblewoman.

Oh personage, oh lady, we (do not wish to) distract you, bring illness upon you, or cause you stomach pains. How is your bodily condition? Are you enjoying a bit of the health of our Lord? Or are some of His afflictions coming upon you? Be of good cheer, my noble person, oh personage, oh lady.

Repondeles ella.

Y.yo nŏxhuīhuān noxōcŏyōhuān nīxquàmōlhuān notēntzŏnhuān: quēnmach huel ōīmàcēhualtic in tlācatl izcihuāpilli: auh in ātl in tĕpētl, inic ye amēchmomănīlia inīc ye amēchmŏzcăltīlia in tlācătl in totēcuiyo in īlhuīcăhuà in tlāltīcpăquè. Cue, noxōcŏyōhuan, intlā oc amīxco amocpac tlachianì in tēteuctin in tlàtòquè, quēzçan yè motlaçòcāmatizquia amēchchōquilīzquia? Quēnnĕl, ca ye īmīcămpa ye [f.9r] īntĕpōtzco in ōamēchmotlācătililì in ōamechmoyōcōlīli in tlachīhuălècātzīntli in tlayōcŏyăni, ye inēncāuhyān in ātl in tĕpētl: Quēn conmonequiltīz in tlōquè in nāhuăquè, àço huel oc cemilhuitzintli amīmàcēhual anyezquè in tlācatl izcihuāpilli nochpōchtzin, yhuan in cuītlăpīlli in àtlapalli. Tlā īxquich amotlàpaltzin xoconmochīhuilīcān: ximìmăticān xitēmahuiztilīcān xitlătlācămătīcān, xitēīmăcăcīcān: auh huel xoconcuīcān xoconānăcān inic anmăchtīlò, inīc

She answers them.

Alas, my grandchildren, my youngest ones, my eyebrows and lip hairs,[3] how fortunate are the lady and the city that our Lord the Master of heaven and earth is letting you grow up so. Oh, my youngest ones, if the lords and rulers (of the past) could see you, how appreciative they would be and how they would cry over you! But what is to be done, the Master of creatures and the Creator caused you to be born and come to life after their time, when they were gone from the city. What will be the desire of the All-pervasive? Perhaps the lady my daughter and the common folk will enjoy you for a whole lifetime. Exert every effort. Be prudent, respectful, obedient, and very cautious. Take to heart what you are taught, how you are admonished and brought up, so that in the future you can get along with people and

annōnōtzălò inic amĭzcăltĭlò; ic huel in mōztla in huīptla tētlŏc tēnāhuac anmonĕmītīzquè, ic huel antēĭtquĭzquè antēmāmāzquè. O, ca īxqui[ch] ic amomātzin amēlchĭquĭuhtzin nicpachoa. Tlā īxquich amotlàpaltzin noxōcŏyōhuān noxhuīhuān.

Responde a la vieja el ayo por los muchachos.

Ōtiquinmocnēlilì in mŏxhuĭuhtzitzinhuān tlācătle cihuāpille nopiltzīntzine, àço quicuizquè àço cānazquè in mìīyōtzin in motlàtōltzin, àço imĭcpăc, àço īnquĕchtlăn, àço īntōzcătlan quitlālīzquè in motōptzinco in mopĕtlācăltzīnco tiquinhuālmoquīxtililia in tlaçòchālchĭhuĭtl in tĕōtētl in māquiztetl: auh in tlaçòihuitl in quĕtzălli inīc tiquinmocnēlilia. Otlaçòtic in moyōllòtzin: ca intlā oc onmoyetztienì in huēhuetquè ĭlămătquè tlàtòquè, cihuāpīpĭltin, ca yèhuān centēntica cĕncămătica quicuĕpăzquià in mìīyōtzin in motlàtōltzin: ōmotlamachtìquè ōimicnōpiltic, tlācătle, cihuāpille.

govern them. Oh, this is all with which I kiss your hands and chests. Be of good cheer, my youngest ones, my grandchildren.

The tutor answers the old woman for the boys.

Your grandchildren owe you thanks, oh personage, oh lady, oh my noble person. Perhaps they will take your words to heart. Perhaps they will place on their heads and at their necks and throats the precious greenstones, the jet, the bracelets that you took from your secret chests and reed baskets, the precious feathers and quetzal plumes you have bestowed upon them (i.e., your words of wisdom). You have been generous. If the men and women of old, the rulers and ladies, were still alive, they would reply to your words with a (fitting) phrase or two. (The children) have been fortunate, oh lady.

Responde la vieja al ayo.

Ō, notēchīuhcāuh otīquinmocnēlilì in moxhuīhuān: tlā īxquich motlàpaltzin xoconmochīhuili: tlā ompōpōhui tlā onixtlāhui in nānyōtl in tàyōtl. Āc huel conchīhuaz conmocuĭtlăhuīz? canel oc cĕmĭlhuītzīntli mitzonmochicāhuilia in ĭlhuĭcăhuà in tlāltĭcpăquê.

La mesma vieja da el parabien a la madre por lograrsele los dos hijos.

Cue, nocihuāpiltzin, quēnmach huel tèhuātzin in ōmitzmomàcēhualtilì in īpalnemōāni in totēchīuhcātzin in totēyōcōxcātzin in tlaçòcōzcămè in tlaçòchālchiuhtin: Ca çā huel mohuēimănà, ca ça huel huēiquiçà [f.9v] in ītlàchīhualhuān in tlācatl in totēcuiyo. Tlā xonmotlachialti in tochān in Mēxìco Tĕnŏchtĭtlan, in Ātzăquălco, nocè in oc īzquĭcān tēcpan, āquin oc mà mozcaltia in tlācati, çā onmomiquilià: Çan ye nō ihui Tlăcōpan

The old woman answers the tutor.

Oh my progenitor, your grandchildren (charges) owe you thanks. Exert all your effort. Let parenthood flourish. Who can manage to be responsible for it (but you), since the Master of heaven and earth is still keeping you healthy for a while.

The same old woman congratulates the mother on her two sons having turned out well.

Ah, my lady, how fortunate are you to whom the Giver of life, our Engenderer and Creator, has given these precious jewels and green stones! The creatures of our Lord are growing very big, turning out very big. Consider our home Mexico Tenochtitlan, Atzaqualco (the place of the dike), or the palaces in all the other places. Hardly anyone who is born grows up, they just die off. It is the same in Tlacopan,

Azcapōtzalco Ĭtz[t]ăpălāpan; O, in īzquĭcān cătè tēpilhuān in oc yelōac: Niman ye in ye nĭci tochān Tĕtzcòco in moyōlcāntzīnco in motlācătĭāntzīnco, ye nō ontlămōa, in àmo çan tlapōhualtin oncatcà tlàtòquè pīpiltin in ītlācăyōhuān in tlācatl moyetzticatca Ācōlmīztli Neçăhuălcŏyōtl, niman yè in xōcŏyōtl Ācatlmāpīchtli Neçăhuălpilli, niman yè in chīchīmēcapīpiltin. In ìquāc nihuālnŏzcălì huel [. . .] centzontli: yhuan quēzqui catca in tēcpīlcalli in intètēcpan pīpiltin tlàtòquè catcà in iuh cē in tēcpancalli, àmo çan tlapōhualtin in tēpilhuān in tēĭxhuīhuān catca: auh àmo onmopōhuăyà in tētlăn nĕnquè mācēhualtin, nocè in tlātlācòtin; yuhquin tzīcătl onoc. Auh in āxcan ye nŏhuĭan motlālpolhuia motlālcănāhuilia in totēcuiyo ye tontlamì ye tipolihuì: tle īca? tle īpampa? àço īçōmāltzin, àço īquălāntzin īpan otiàquè, ic ōtictoteòpōhuilìquè in totlàtlăcōl in totlăpīlchīhual.

Azcapotzalco, and Itztapalapan, wherever there were nobles living (in the past). Here in our home of Texcoco, your birthplace, things are also coming to an end. There were innumerable rulers and nobles who were relatives of the former lord Acolmiztli Nezahualcoyotl, and also the son, Acamapichtli Nezahualpilli, and the (other) Chichimeca nobles. Back when I was growing up, there was an infinite number of them. And how many noble houses there were, the palaces of the former nobles and rulers! It was like one big palace. There were countless (minor) nobles and lesser relatives, and one could not count the commoners who were dependents, or the slaves;[4] they were like ants. But now everywhere our Lord is destroying and reducing the land. We are coming to an end and disappearing. Why? For what reason? Perhaps

Quēnnel, canel tītlăchīhualhuān ca tītlăyōcoxhuān, ca īcenmāctzinco ticatè, ca totēchīuhcātzin ca totēyōcoxcātzin, quēn techonmonequililīz in mōztla in huīptla, tlā tictotlàtōlchialīcān: Mā yè īxquich totlàpal toconchīhuacān inic titlācahuapāhuà inīc titlācăzcăltià: mā ompōpōhui mā onixtlāhui in nānyōtl in tàyōtl: mā huel oncuitlahuiltilōcān in topilhuān in totzŏnhuān in toztĕhuān in yēcyōtl in quăllōtl, inic huel quimīmăcăxīlīzquè quimotlayecoltilīzquè in tlācatl in totēcuiyo in tlŏquè in nāhuăquè; īhuan inīc huel īhuian yōcoxcā tētlŏc tēnāhuac onnemizquè, īlhuĭz in āxcan, ca cencà huel ye monequi inīc huel necuĭltlăhuīlōzquè: yèīca ca ye cencà huēiya tlăpīhuĭa in àquallōtl in àyēcyōtl in tlahuelilōcāyōtl, ye huel īntech tlăquāhua, niman īmpilpēhuăyān pēhuà in aoc quēn momatì in aocmo tlătlācamatì, in aoctle oncà inpīnāhuiz.

we have incurred His wrath and offended Him with our sins and wrongdoing. But what are we to do? Since we are His creatures and entirely in His hands and He is our Engenderer and Creator, let us await His command as to what His will will be for us in the future. Let us do all we can to raise up children; let parenthood flourish. Let our children, our offspring, be made to look after the proper and good so that they will truly fear and serve our Lord the All-pervasive, and so that they can live peacefully among other people; especially today they greatly need to be well looked after, because evil and bad behavior are greatly growing, increasing, and hardening in them. Hardly are they born when they begin not to care about anything, not to obey, to have no shame.

Prosigue y cuenta como se criavan los hijos antiguamente en su gentilidad.

In ìquāc nihuālnŏzcălì in tlàtòquè īmpilhuān in ŏquĭchpīpiltŏtōtin [f.10r] ōmpa in machitilōyan in izcaltilōyà in Tlācătēcco, huel quinmonòmàhuiliāyà in tlācătl Tĕcuĕpòtzin Cihuācōātzīntli, ȳhuān in āchcāuhtlămăcăzqui in huēy tlămăcăzqui: niman yè in quĕtzălcōātl: huel ìquāc in yŏhuălli xĕlĭhuĭa quimēhuăyà, nohuian tlăàhuăchĭà tlăchpānà: niman ic onēhuà in ōmpa quăuhtēnco conmāmāyà in ăcxŏyătl in ŏcŏpĕtlătl inīc tlachìchīhuāyà. Inon cuix ye cuēl totècuiyo ichāntzīnco? ca çan oc tlācătĕcŏlōtl ītĕòcalco catca, àço Tēzcăcatlĕpōca* nocè Huītzĭlōpōchtli, Tlāloc īhuān oc cĕquīn ĭztlăcătētĕò catcà tlātlācătĕcŏlò; niman ic mopàpācà màāltià: mānel yè cencà cēhua.

* Virtually every other source without diacritics has *Tezcatlipoca*.

She continues and tells how children were raised in the old days, in pagan times.

Back when I was brought up, the boys who were children of rulers were taught and raised at the Tlacatecco (a temple school).[5] The lord Tecuepochtzin, the Cihuacoatl,[6] and the senior priest, the great priest, themselves saw to them, and also the Quetzalcoatl (a priest). They (the adults in charge) got them up right at midnight. They (the children) sprinkled and swept everywhere. Next they left for the edge of the woods and carried fir and ferns with which they decorated (the temples). Now was that already the house of our Lord? They were still just demons' temples of Tezcatlipoca, Huitzilopochtli, or Tlaloc, and of other demons who were false gods.[7] Next they washed and bathed themselves, even though it was very cold. And by the time it had cleared and become full day, they had

Auh in ye ōtlătlālchipāhuac in ye tlàcà ō nŏhuĭan tlăcècencāuhquè inic tlăchìchīhua. Niman ye cēcĕntetl, noço intlā yè ăchi huèhuēin tlăxcălçŏlli tlālpan quinhuāllāxilia, yuhquin chĭchĭtzĭtzin īpan quinmatì. Auh in ōŏntēnìçăquè, ic pēhuà in quinmachtià in iuh nĕmĭzquè in iuh tlătlācăma-tizquè in iuh tēmahuiztilīzquè in quimomăcăzquè in quallōtl in yēcyōtl, auh inīc quitlālcāhuīzquè in īxpampa ēhuazquè in àquallōtl in àyēcyōtl in tlăhuēlĭlōcāyōtl in tlācăçolyōtl. Quēxquich ōncān quicuià cānayà in īxtlămăchiliztli in nèmătīliz-tli: auh inīc tlatzăcuīltĭlōyà, intlā ītlà tĕpĭtōn ōquìtlăcòquè cencà tēīçahuì tēmàmauhtì: quim-pĭloāyà quinchilpŏpōchhuiāyà, quintzītzĭcāzhuià quintlăcōhuītĕquì, īncōtz inmŏlĭc, īnnăcăztĭtech mĕhuĭztli càăquĭāya, quinquātlĕcŏtŏtzŏà quin-tlàtlătià. Auh çan ye nō ihui in nepantlà tōnătĭuh, in ìquāc huel mopītza in tōnatiuh, quimonīhuà in quăuhtēnco: quăhuĭtl tlăxīpēhualli ŏcŏtl in

prepared the decorations everywhere. Then they (the adults) threw down on the ground to them (the children) an old tortilla each, or perhaps (more) if they were a little larger. They treated them like little dogs. And when they had breakfasted, they (the adults) began teaching them how to live, how to obey, and how to honor people, to give themselves to the good and to relinquish and shun evil, bad behavior, and excess. How much wisdom and prudence they absorbed there! And as to how they were punished, if they did the least thing wrong, it was very frightening: they hanged them up, they set them in the smoke of burning chiles, they hit them with nettles and beat them with switches on their calves and elbows. They stuck maguey spines in their ears, they put their heads close to the fire and scorched them. And likewise at midday, when the sun was very hot, they sent them to the edge

conmāmāyà: huel ìhuì in netlălōlo tŏtōcōa: ăyāc māhuiltia, nocè tētōtŏpēuhtiuh, mochtīn mìmatcātlăloà, momăuhtìtihuì, tlăīmăcăztĭhuì: auh çan cuēl ăchīc in huālmocuĕpà. Auh in ōàcicò oc ceppa çan ye nō ihui inīc quintlămăcà, çan tlālpan quintlāxilià cēcĕntl [*sic*] nŏcè òōmĕ in tlăxcălçŏlli inic motlàcàhuià. Auh in ōontlăquàquè, niman ye ic oc ceppa pēhuà in quinmachtià: nō cuēl yè izcĕquīn in quēnin mìcălizquè, nocè in quēnin àāmĭzquè, inic tlătlàcălhuāzhuīzquè, nocè inic tlămōtlazquè, moch ic momachtià in chīmălli in mācquăhuĭtl; auh in mītl in tlătzŏn[tec]tli àtlătica ic motlāça. Niman yè inīc tlămātlăhuīlo tlatzŏnhuāzhuĭlo. Oc cĕquīn yè in nepāpan tōltēcăyōtl măchtilò in [f.10v] āmăntēcăyōtl ìhuitl quĕtzălli ic mochìchīhua: niman yè in xiuhçālōliztli in teōcuitlapītzaliztli in chālchĭuhtlătĕquiliztli, tlăpĕtlāhualitztli, niman yè in tlàcuilōliztli, quăuhxīmaliztli, īhuān in oc cequi nepāpan tōltēcăyōtl. Oc cĕquīn yèhuātl in

of the woods. They (the children) carried wood, bark, and kindling. They ran energetically. No one idled or went along shoving people down; all ran prudently and went with fear and respect, and in a very short while they returned. And when they (the children) had arrived again, they (the adults) fed them the same way. They just threw down on the ground to them one or two old tortillas each, with which they had their mid-day meal. And when they had eaten, right away they (the adults) began teaching them again: again (resuming from the morning), to some how to do battle, or how to hunt, how to shoot a blow-gun or how to hurl stones. They were taught all about the shield and the hand sword, and how to hurl spears and darts with a spear thrower; also about netting and snaring. Others were taught the different crafts: feather work, how (small) feathers and quetzal plumes were

machtilò in cuīcapīquiliztli in tlàtōlpèpĕnăliztli in tlămăchīliztli in mìtoa motēnēhua huēhuētl ăyăcāchtli: niman yè in ilhuicatlămătīliztli, in iuh molīnia in tōnatiuh in mētztli ihuān izcīcītlaltin in mìtoa chiucnāuhnĕpăniuhqui: niman yè in motēnēhua tĕōāmōxtli in ītechpatzinco ic tlàtōāya in tlŏquè nāhuăquè in tēyōcŏyăni: àtēl nō īhuān in īntechpa in ĭztlăcătētĕò catcà inic netlăpŏlōltilōya, canel oc yŏhuăyān catca, ca ăyămo īmpan huālàcic in ītlănēxtzin in tlācatl in totēcuiyo in tlănĕltŏquīliztli; nĕl cĕquīn quimonhuīcà in mīlpan, nŏcè in xòxōchitlà inic quinmachitiāyà in quēnin tōcazque quăuhăquīzquè xōchĭăquĭzquè, nŏcè ēlĭmĭquĭzquè tlătlālhuīzquè. Moch quinmachitiāya in īxquich quēxquich monequia quimătĭzquè in tlatĕquĭpănōliztli in tlămăchīliztli in īxtlămătīliztli in nèmatcānemiliztli. Çan ye nō ihui in calìtic in ōmpa moyetzticatcà izcihuāpīpīltin in īnyĕyāntzīnco ōmpa

arranged (to make shields, etc.), also mosaic work, gold-smithery, jewel cutting, and metal polishing; and also (codex?) painting, woodworking, and the various other crafts. Others were taught song composition and oratory and the science known as "the drum and the rattle" (i.e., music), and also the science of the heavens, how the sun and moon and stars, called the Ninefold, move; and then what are called divine codices, which talked about the All-pervasive, the Creator of humanity, though they also were about the former false gods with whom people used to delude themselves, for it was still the time of darkness, and the light of our Lord, the faith, had not yet reached them. And they took some (students) to the fields or the flower gardens to teach them how to sow seeds, to plant trees and flowers, and to cultivate and work the land. They taught them all it was needful for

machtilōyà in īchpōpōchtin in īxquich in nepāpan cihuāyeliztli in tlăchpānaliztli in tlăàhuăchīlĭztli tlăquălchìchīhuăliztli, āchīhualiztli, tĕxĭliztli, tlăxcălmănăliztli tămălōliztli, in īxquich nĕpāpăn cĭhuāpan mochìchīhuani. Niman yè in mălăcătl tzŏtzŏpāztli nepāpan tlàmăchtli: niman yè in tlăpāliztli ic mopāya nepāpan tlăpălli tōchìhuitl, mìtōa tōchòmitl. Auh çan ye nō ihui inīc cencà tlatzăcuīltĭlōyà in āquìquè ītlà quìtlăcŏāya in àmo motlăcuĭtlăhuiāyà: auh huel necuĭtlăhuīlōyà: ăyāc huel ăcà ōmpa călăquià in ŏquĭchtin, huel īnyòcă catca ĭlămătquè cĭhuāpīpīltin quinmocuĭtlăhuià: auh năuhpōhualtica in ōnhuĭà in ōmpa tlācătēcco in concăquĭà in īnāuhpōhuallàtōl in tlācătl tlàtoāni Ācōlmiztli Necăhuălcŏyōtzin, in ōncān quinmonōnōchiliaya quinmàhuiliāya in tlācatl Tĕcuĕpòtzin. Auh çan ye nō ihui inīc mozcaltiāyà in mācēhuăltzĭtzīntin in tēlpōchpīpĭltŏtōntin,

them to know by way of service, knowledge, wisdom, and prudent living. Likewise within the houses, where the ladies were in their quarters, the girls were taught all the different things women do: sweeping, sprinkling, preparing food, making beverages, grinding (maize), preparing tortillas, making tamales, all the different things customarily done among women; also the spindle and the weaver's reed (stick) and various kinds of embroidery; also dyeing, how rabbit down or rabbit fur was dyed different colors. And in the same way (as with the boys) those who did something wrong or did not take care were severely punished. And they were all well cared for: no men, no matter who, entered there; taking care of them was the exclusive domain of the elderly noblewomen. And every eighty days they went to the Tlacatecco and heard the

ōmpa in ĭzcăltĭlōyà in cămlĕcăc tēlpōchcăli[*]: auh izcihuāpīpĭltŏtōntin ōmpa izcĭhuātĕōpan, in ōmpa tzāuctĭcatcà cĭhuātlămàcēuhquè moçăuhquè. Ō, ca ihui yn in ōnĕmicò in ōtlămănīltīcò in huēhuetquè tēchmocāhuilìtihuì: çā cencà huēy[†] inīc ōmŏtlăcuĭtlăhuīcò. Auh in āxcan ye huel oc centlamantli inic tiquinhuăpāhuà to- [f.11r] pilhuān aocmo mīmăcăcì in tlăhuĕlīlōcāyōtl, yèīca inīc aocmo quīmăcăcì in tētlăxxīmălĭztli in ĭchtĕquĭliztli in tlāhuānălĭztli, ȳhuān in oc cequi tlahuelīlōcāyōtl, īpampa in aocmo yuh tētzăcuīltilo, in iuh ōtētzăcuīltĭlōya in oc ye huècāuh in niman ic tēmĕcānĭlōya tēpòpŏlōlōya: ca huel oc niquittac ca nīxpan mochīuh, in ìquāc tētlaxxīn in tlācatl Āxāyăcătzin Mēxìco Tĕnŏchtitlan tlàtoāni

* This is the first of two places where *calli*, the word for "house" is spelled with only a single "l."

† This is the one place in the manuscript where there appears to be a redundant breve over a "y."

eighty-day speech of the lord ruler Acolmiztli Nezahualcoyotl,[8] and there the lord Tecuepotzin admonished them and cautioned them. And the commoners were raised in the same way; the youths were raised in the school at the youths' house, and the girls at the women's temple, where the female penitents were enclosed and fasted. Oh, this is how the ancients who left us behind lived and ordered things; they took very great care. Bad behavior is no longer feared, for they no longer fear adultery, theft, drunkenness, and other kinds of bad behavior, because it is no longer punished as it used to be punished long ago, when they forthwith garroted and destroyed people. For I even saw it myself and it happened before my eyes, when the daughter of the lord Axayacatl, ruler of Mexico Tenochtitlan, committed adultery with Maxtla of the house of Tezayuca and with Huitzilihuitl, that it

ichpōchtzin, īhuān in căli [*sic*] tēçōnyòcān Māxtla, īhuān Huītzīlìhuitl, ca cencà huel huēy in mochīuh, ca àmo çan tlăpōhualtin in quitzăuctiàquè, in īhuān cihuāpilli mĕcānīlōquè tētĕpăchōlōquè, cĕquīn călpīxquè, cĕquin tōltēcà, cĕquīn pōchtēcà: niman yè in īpìhuān, īhuān in ītlănnĕncāhuān izcihuāpilli, centlālli mŏmăn, nŏhuĭān āhuàcān tĕpēhuàcān huālhuīlōac in tlămăhuĭçōcò, quinhuālhuīcăquè izcihuāpīpīltin in īmichpōchhuān; inmānel yè cōçŏlco ŏnŏquè, inīc quintlachialtìquè: inmānel yè Tlăxcăltēcà Huĕxōtzincà Ātlīx[c]à in toyāōhuān catcà, huel oc moch tlăchĭăcò, huel tètēn in īxquich chōlōltēcăcālli in tlăpăntli. Auh inīc tētlăquăltì in tlācatl tlàtoāni Nĕçăhuălpīltzīntli moch tlatzīncŏyōnīlli in ācăchĭquĭhuitl in mōlcăxĭtl: huel ic mopīnāuhtìquè in Mēxìcà: auh çan ye nō ihui niquittac inic conmomĕcānīlìquè in tlācătl Huĕxōtzīncătzin in īyăcăpăn catca tlācătl tlàtoāni Neçăhuălpiltzīntli: izçan huel iyò

was done on a grand scale and countless people were punished, who were garroted and crushed with stones along with the lady: some stewards, some artisans, and some merchants, and also the ladies-in-waiting and dependents of the lady.[9] All the world assembled. People came from the towns all around to behold. The ladies brought along their daughters, even if they were still in the cradle, to have them see (as a lesson). Even the Tlaxcalans, and the people of Huexotzinco and Atlixco, although they were our enemies, all came to see. The whole roof of the house of the Cholulans[10] was brimful. And as to how the lord ruler Nezahualpilli fed people, there were all the containers with hollow bases, the reed baskets, and the sauce bowls, by which the Mexica were very much put to shame.[11] And likewise I saw how they garroted the lord Huexotzincatzin, who was the eldest son of the

conmotzăcuīltìtia inīc quimocuīcăpīquĭlĭlì in Tōllan cihuāpilli in īchāhuănāntzin izcihuāhuān tlācătl: auh huālmŏtzăuc in ītēcpanchāntzīnco, quimotōcāyōtĭlì in tlācătl Nĕçăhuălpĭlli in tēcpancălli īxxāyōc, īpampa izçencà quimochōquililì in īmiquiz ītlaçòpiltzin. Çan ye no ihui niquittac inic conmotzacuiltìtià in Quāuhtlĭztāctzin izçan huel ītēīccāuhtzin Huĕxōtzīncătzin izçan ĭyò īpampa monòmàhuìtzinò mocăltìtzīnò in àmo ītēncopa in tlācatl: ȳhuān oc cequīn oniquimittac in pīpiltin, īhuan cihuāpīpiltin in niman ōquimotzăcuīltìtiàquè in tlein ōquimìtlăcălhuìquè: niman yē yèhuan āltĕpēpan tlàtòquè. O in Quauhtitlan Tzŏtzŏmàtzin tlāhuānăliztli in conmotzăcuiltìtià. Intlā moch iz ōniquintēnēhuani, ca huel huècāuh in ōntlamizquia ic nitlănōnōtzaz. Auh inin nocihuāpiltzin, mā çā huel onnecuĭtlăhuīlōcān in toxhuīhuān, ca ohuìcān in tlālticpac ōnmātōyāhuīzquè ōnmŏtĕpèxĭhuīzquè;

lord ruler Nezahualpilli; he was punished just for composing songs to the lady of Tollan (Tula), his stepmother, one of the wives of the lord.[12] And he (Nezahualpilli) came back and shut himself up in his palace; the lord Nezahualpilli named the palace "the place of tears," because he wept greatly over the death of his beloved son. Likewise I saw how Cuauhtliztactzin, younger brother of Huexotzincatzin, was punished just because he built himself a residence of his own, not by the order of the lord.[13] And I saw other noblemen and ladies whose wrongdoings were forthwith punished, as well as the rulers of cities (subject to Texcoco). Tzotzomatzin of Cuauhtitlan was punished for drunkenness. If I mentioned all of them here, it would be a very long time before I finished telling it. And so, my lady, let our grandchildren be very well taken care of, for the world is a difficult place.

nocè niman ye quimŏnmocnīuhtià ăcàmè tēlpōchtlăhuĕlīlōquè, ītlà īntech ōntlămiz contzăuctiāzquè. Mā huel īxquich notlàpaltzin xoconmochīhuili notēcuiyo cĭhuātl nocĭhuāpiltzin, tlaçòtli tlācătzintli.

Responde la Madre a la Vieja.

[f.11v] Otiquinmocnēlilì in momācēhualtŏtōnhuān, quēn conmonĕquīltiz in tlācătl in totēcuiyo, àço huel mozcăltīzquè, àço huel mohuăpāhuazquè, auh ànŏcè ye iz tlantihuītz in ītēilnāmĭquĭliztzin in tlācatl in totēcuiyo in cŏcŏliztli, àço çan yè ic quimonmopòpŏlhuīz quimonmotlàtlātilīz. Ca īxquich notlàpal noconchīhua inīc niquimŏnnŏcuĭtlăhuia; īhuān in tlācătl izcihuāpilli ca nō īxquich ītlàpaltzin quimochīhuilia huel ōquinmomāmăltilì in motēchīuhcāuh in Antontzin Cōhuātēcătzintli, huel quimitzti-

They may fall into the river or from a precipice (i.e., get into serious trouble); they may make friends with some delinquent boys and they will be accused of something and punished. Make every effort, oh my mistress and lady, oh precious personage.

The mother answers the old woman.

Your little vassals owe you thanks. What will be the will of our Lord? Perhaps they will be able to grow up; but perhaps the remembrance of our Lord, illness, will strike us, perhaps in that way He will destroy and remove them from view.[14] I exert all my effort to take care of them, and the lady (their grandmother) also exerts all her effort. And Antonio Coatecatl, your progenitor, has really taken them upon himself. He goes about looking after them and taking good care of them, for raising children

nemi huel quinmocuĭtlăhuìtinemi; ca ye īxcocà in tlācăhuăpāhuăliztli in tlācăzcăltĭliztli, quēzquīn in ye quinmŏzcăltilia pīpiltin notlàtzĭtzīnhuān, niman yè in nĭŭctzin [*sic*] ō nō quimŏzcăltilì; çan huel yèhuātl in yăcăpăntōntli achi nēchtĕquĭpăchŏa in ăchi cuèciuhqui in niman àmo tlăīmăcăci in ō nō chĭpĕtōntēhuac, yuhquin mà chīchīmēcatl motēnhuītectĭuh tzàtzĭtĭuh in motlălŏa: auh àcan mà moquetza, niman huèca yăuh chŏlŏa, in quēmman Tĕtzcòco in conānà: nĕl cănà oc huèca āltĕpētl īpan: immānel yè nicmĕcăxīpēhua nicchīlpŏpōchhuĭa, nocè oc huālcà ic nictolīnia nictòtōnēhua izçā micqui niccāhua, niman àmo ic tlăcăquiznĕqui.

Replica la Vieja.

Àmo nel yuhqui ītōnal nocihuāpiltzin, mitzmotŏlīnilia, àço quimoquīxtilì in īāchcòcōltzin in tlācatl Ȳxtlīlxōchitzin, ca huel yuhcātzintli moyetzticatca.

is his special domain. How many of my noble uncles did he raise? And he also raised my little brother. But especially (my) little first-born concerns me somewhat. He's quite mischievous and afraid of nothing at all, and when he has (flown out of the house?) he runs howling and shouting as though he were a Chichimec.[15] He stops nowhere, and right away goes running far off. Sometimes they catch him in Texcoco, or even somewhere in cities farther away. Though I skin his hide with a rope and stick him in chile smoke or hurt and afflict him even more and leave him practically dead, he won't listen at all.

The old woman replies.

Such is not his destiny, my lady. It bothers you (needlessly). Perhaps he takes after his great-grandfather the lord Ixtlilxochitl, for he was just like that.

Avisos para comer con buena criança.

Notēlpōchtze amechmonōchiliā in tlācatl, anmotlaqualtītīhuì. Xiquittacān in quēnin ancalaquì, çan pani in huālmotzilìticà in tlācătl: ximìmattihuiān: īxpantzīnco amonmopĕchtēcà anconmotlàpalhuia. Auh inic antlaquāzquè, àmo oncān ximīxcuelitztiecān ximàhuatiecān: ȳhuān àmo çan tlalhuiz xitlăquācān, ximoxìxicuinōcān, çan īhuiān, īhuān àmo xicpēpetztŏlòtihuetzicān in tlein anquiquāzquè izçan màāntiuh anquitŏloà, huel oc xicquăquācān, īhuan àmo ixachchi in anquicācămatēmà, çan tepitzitzin in anquicuitihuì inic huel anquiquāzquè. Auh in ìquāc mōlāyōtl anquiltĕquizquè, nocè ātl anconīzquè, àmo xiìcicatocān. cuix anchĭchĭmè çan yōlic, īhuān àmo mochi īca in amomàpil, çan iyò in ètĕtl amomàpil, ȳhuān īca in amoyēcmā: ȳhuān mācamo oncān pìpilcatie in amoyacatolcuitl, ximoyăcăpòpōhuacān:

An adult's *advice* to the boys *for eating with good breeding.*

My sons, the lord is summoning you to dine. Look how you enter, for the lord is (right there?) looking this way. Go prudently, bow down before him and greet him. And when you eat, don't be making angry faces and squabbling, and don't eat carelessly and gorge yourselves, but delicately. And don't let the food just slide down your throats, but swallow at intervals. Keep chewing, and don't stuff your mouths, but take just little morsels so you will chew them well. And when you are sipping soup or drinking water, don't be slurping—are you dogs?—but (drink) quietly, and don't use all your fingers, but only three of them, and use your right hand. And don't let your snot be hanging down; wipe your noses. And don't be throwing things down and spitting, you'll disgust people. And I warn you

yhuan àmo xitlatlăztocān xi- [f.12r] chìchatocān, antētlàyeltīzque. Oc in iz moch namēchnèmachtia: mānēn ītlà anquìtlacòtin, in ōmpa ca tēīxpan. Tlein huel oc tamēchilhuīzquè? àmo cencà tēpīnāuhtì? Quēn amìtōlōzquè? ihuān quēn tìtōlōzquè in tēcpan ōtitozcaltìquè? Yhuān in ìquāc ōanmotlālìquè in oncān tlăqualōyān àmo niman xiccuitihuetzicān in tlaqualli: oc acattopa xicteōchīhuacān xitlătlātlăuhtīcān. Auh intlā ācà oncān amonāhuac tlăquāz, mā yèhuātl oc acattopa pēhua in tlăquāz. Intlā ōmotlapōlolti in motìtītlani tētlaqualtia, intlā cēmè amèhuān acattopa ōamēchmanilīto tlaqualli, mōlli; īxpan xoconìquanīcān in āquin amohuan tlaqua. Intlā nel yè çan amonehuān, intlā tè titētēiccāuh mīxpan acattopa ōquimanato xoconìquanili in motiāchcătzin. Xitēmahuiztilīcān, ximomahuiztilīcān, ca moch quimotztilìticà in tlācătl: auh in tlein amèhuān anquìtlacoà oc tèhuān acattopa tamēchcuĭtlătzăquà

all here, don't do anything wrong, for you are in public there. What more can I tell you? Is it not very shameful? What will people say about you? And what will people say about us who were raised at court? And when you have taken your place in the dining room, don't hurry right away to take the food; first bless it and pray. And if someone is to eat next to you,[16] let him begin eating first. If the person sent to wait on people has made a mistake and offered food and sauce to one of you first, move it over in front of the person eating with you. Even if it should be just one of you, if you are the younger and (the servant) has placed (the food) before you first, move it over to your elder. Be respectful to people and to each other, for the lord observes everything, and for what you do wrong we are the ones who first take the blame. He (the lord) scolds us on account of you and says we are not taking care

amopampa techmàhuilia quimìtalhuia in àmo tamēchtocuitlahuià in àmo tamēchnōnōtzà tamēchtlăcāhualtià, ō, tlā xicalaquicān.

Lo que dicen despues de comer à su Madre dos niños.

Ōtlăcāuhqui in iyōllòtzin totēcuiyo nopiltzīntzine cihuāpille, ca īhuiān yōcoxcā ō motechtzinco monec in tlamātzoaltzintli in ātĕxātzintli: auh ōtomàcēhualtic ōtocnōpiltic in īcŏcōcàtzin in tlācatl in totēcuiyo: mā cencà ic tictoyēctēnēhuilīcan. Auh ōtitēchmocnēlilì tlācătle cihuāpille nopiltzintzine.

Quēn ōticmotlathuitì, quēn ōmitzmotlathuitilì in tlācatl in totēcuiyo? cuix tepitzin ticmomàcēhuìtzinoa in ītēchchicāhualiztzin? cuix nocè ītlà ītēmoxtzin ièēcatzin mopantzinco quihuālmihuāliznequi? canel àmo ticmatì inīc techmonemītilia in ītlālticpactzinco in ilhuicahuà in tlālticpaquè in īpalnemoani.

of you, not reprimanding and restraining you. Now go on in.

What two boys say to their mother after eating.

Our Lord has been generous, my noble lady; in peace the food and drink have been consumed at your table. The goods of our Lord have been our good fortune; let us greatly praise Him for it. Thank you, oh personage, oh lady, oh my noble person.

A boy greets his uncle.

How did you feel on rising? How did our Lord cause you to feel on rising? Are you enjoying a bit of His health? Or is He about to send some of His afflictions upon you? For we do not know how the Master of heaven and earth, the Giver of life, is causing you to fare on His earth.

R[a.]

Otinechmocnēlilì nomăchtze: mācihui in ōninohuēhuètilì izçā nihuìhuĭtōntinemi in ītlālticpactzinco in tlācatl in totēcuiyo: tel achìtzin nichuelmati in tlālli izçŏquĭtl, īhuan huel onyauh in ātĕxātzīntli in tlamātzohualtzintli nechmomaquilia māhuitzin.

Dos viejos principals saludan à unos Cantores.

Anmotolīnià noxōcŏyōhuāne, ōaquìiyōhuìquè: àço ōti[c]tlàcàtilìquè tlā çā yè pēhua in huēhuētl, ic huālìçaz in tlācatl, canīcīpac* in cuīcatl.
[f.12v]

* This seems to have been a copying error. It was probably originally something on the order of "ca īc pāqui," given the governor's statement on folio 12v, and a similar statement found in Chimalpahin's Seventh Relation.

Reply.

Thank you, my nephew. Though I have grown old and am just tottering along on our Lord's earth, still I am tolerably well in body, and the food and drink your aunt gives me agree with me.

Two elderly noblemen greet some singers in the morning.

You are suffering (standing here waiting), oh my youngest ones, greetings. Perhaps we have caused things to be behind schedule. Just let the drum begin, with which the lord will awaken, for (he takes joy in?) song.

Responden los cantores.

Nopiltzintzine tlàtoānie ōanquimìȳyōhuiltìque, cĕcuĭztli amotlantzinco aqui, ca qualcān in ōanmàxitīcò, ca çā oc achi yohuatōnco, quin ye huālmoquetza in tlāhuizcalli, auh in tlācatl mocēhuìtzinòtoc: ōtontlàtlăcaquito in īyĕyāntzinco, tlamattimani, ayāc mà nāhuati: ȳhuān in tōpīlèquè calìtic motlacuitlahuia, ayamo quihuāllapoà. Quēn yè ōamechmotlathuiltilì in totēcuiyo? cuix tepitzin yēctli qualli ōanquimomàcēhuìtzinòque in iiyohualtzin.* cuix nocè ītlà ītēmoxtzin īèēcatzinco ō amopantzinco ōquihuālmihuālì? canel àmo ticmatì inīc òtlatoca in yohualli in tlàcàtli in īcemilhuitzin in tlācatl in totēcuiyo, nopiltzintzine, cocoliztli tamēchtocuītilīzque: Mā yè nicān ximohuetziltīcan in amoyeyāntzinco in amocpalpantzinco.

* This word should begin with a single "ī."

The singers answer.

Oh my nobleman, oh ruler, greetings. You must be cold. You have arrived in good time, for it's still quite early. Dawn has just come, and the lord lies resting. We have listened around his quarters, and it's quiet, no one's talking, and the officials who take care of things in the house haven't come yet to open up. How did the Lord cause you to feel on rising? Did you enjoy His night rather well, or did He send something of His afflictions down upon you? For we do not know how our Lord's day, both nighttime and daytime, marches along. We (do not wish to) make you ill; do sit down here in your places, your seats.

Ohua nŏxōcŏyōhuāne ōannechmocnēlilìquè, auh ōanquimocnēlilìquè in nomachtzin: ca tepitzin quēntēltzin ōtēchmohuēytlathuiltilì in tlācatl in totēcuiyo in īpalnemoāni, ca tepitzin tictomàcēhuià in ītēchcāhualiztzin.

Unos principales saludã à su Gov^or.
Despues de levantado de la cama aviendo cantado antes à su modo.

Tlācatle, tlàtoānie timitzontonepechtēquililià, àço ōtimitztotzonteconēhuilìquè: quēn ōmitzmotlathuiltilì in tlācatl in totēcuiyo? cuix tepitzin huel onyà in cochiztli? canel miec inic conàmana in mixtzin in moyōllòtzin in ītcōca in īmāmalōca in ātl in tepētl. Tlā īxquich motlàpaltzin xoconmochīhuili, tlā onixtlāhui, tlā ompōpohui tēucyōtl in tlàtòcāyōtl, auh in nānyōtl in tàyōtl. Ca ye imman in, àço toconmāniliz in mocxitzin, inic tonmohuīcaz īchāntzinco totēcuiyo: ca ye iz moch mitzmochialìtoquè in motēchīuhcāhuan.

Reply.

Ah, my youngest ones, I thank you on my behalf and on behalf of my nephew here. Our Lord the Giver of life caused us to rise tolerably well, and we are enjoying a bit of His health.

Some noblemen greet their governor after he has risen from his bed, first having sung to him in their fashion.

O personage, oh ruler, we bow down to you; we (hope we have not) given you a headache (with our singing). Did your sleep go rather well? For you disturb your spirit greatly with the governance of the city. Exert all your effort. Let lordship, rulership and parenthood be as they should be. It is late, take to your feet to go to the house of our Lord, for all your progenitors (aides) are here awaiting you.

Respondeles el Gov^or.

Ōannēchmocnēlilìquè nopiltzintzine: ōtlăcāuhqui in amoyōllòtzin: ca tepitzin ōnomàcēhualtic in ītēchicāhualiztzin totēcuiyo. Auh huel ōnonnotlamachtì, huel ic ōnompāc inīc ōnichuālcactoca ōanconmēhuilìquè yāōcuīcatl ic pŏyōmicquè Ācōlhuàquè tlaxcallan yāōtĕpānco, ye achi quēxquich cāhuitl in niquelēhuia noconcaquiz. Auh in yè amèhuantzitzin anmotolīnìtzinoà, àço cĕcuiztli amotlantzinco ăqui, ca oc yohuac in ōanhuālmohuīcaque, yhuan ca inic cēhuatoc. Cuix nō achìtzin anquimomàcēhuìtzinoà in ītēchicāhualiztzin in tloquè nā- [f.13r] huăquè in īpalnemoāni? cuix nocè cēmè amopantzinco quihualmihuālia in ītĕtzin in īquăuhtzin in ītēmoxtzin in īèēcatzin?

Responde uno por todos.

Otitēchmocnēlilì nopiltzintzine tlàtoānie, ca timochtin tocepaniān oc quēntēltzin tocontomàcēhuià in ītēicnēliltzin in tlācatl totēcuiyo.

The governor answers them.

Thank you, oh my noblemen, you have spoken generous words. I have enjoyed a bit of the health of our Lord. And I truly enjoyed and rejoiced in lying listening to you sing the war song about the Acolhuaque dying by treachery at the Tlaxcallan war boundary.[17] For some time now I have been wanting to hear it. You are suffering (standing here). Perhaps you are getting cold, for you came early, and it is chilly. Are you also enjoying a bit of the health of the All-pervasive, the Giver of life? Or has He sent down upon one of you His punishments and afflictions?

One answers him for all.

Thank you, oh my nobleman, oh ruler, we all jointly are tolerably enjoying the beneficence of our Lord.

El Gov$^{or.}$ y Principales saludan à su Guardian.

Notlaçòmahuiztàtzine ca iz ōniquinhuālhuīcac in mopilhuān pīpiltin, tictēnnāmiquicò in motlaçòteōpixcāmātzin, yhuān ticmaticò àço tepitzin yēctli qualli ic ōmitzmìxitilì in tlācatl totēcuiyo; auh ànocè ītlà huālēhuaznequi in ītēmoxtzin in īèēcatzin: ca huel àmo toconmatì inīc ītlālticpactzinco tinemì: ca çan yèhuātl inic timitztonepechtēquililià notlaçòtàtzine.

Guardiã

Ōtinēchmocnēlilì tlàtoānie, yhuān ōnēchicnēlìquè in nopilhuān, ca tēl tepitzin yectli ic ōnēchmotlathuiltilì in totēcuiyo, ca tepitzin nichuelmati in nonacayo. Auh in tèhuātzin quēn nō ticmomachiltia in monaca[yō]tzin; yhuān in mochtīn nopilhuān cuix moch pācticatê?

The governor and noblemen greet the prior of the Franciscan monastery of their town.

Oh my precious revered father, I have brought here your children, the noblemen. We have come to kiss your precious priestly hands and to find out if our Lord caused you to feel rather well on waking, or if some of His afflictions are coming (upon you), for we do not know how we live on His earth. This is all with which we bow down to you, my precious father.

The prior.

I thank you, ruler, and I thank my children, but our Lord caused me to feel rather good on rising, and I am rather well in body. And you, too, how are you in body, and all my children, are they healthy?[18]

Gov[or.]

Ōtocēpanmàcēhualtic notlaçòmahuiztàtzine in motēcatlàtlaniliztzin ca timochtin no tepitzin tēchmomaquilia in īcemilhuitzin in īpalnemoani teōtl Dios.

El escrivano del pueblo saluda à un principal y juez.

Tlācătle tlàtoānie cocoliztli ticmocuītiz melchiquiuhtzin noconēhuaz nictequipachōz in tēucyōtl in tlàtòcāyōtl, nimitzonnocāhualtiliz in āmoyahualli in tlamātzoalli nimitzonnotlapololtiliz nimitznotlalcāhualtiliz in ītechpa in itcōca in īmāmalōca in ātl in tĕpētl: ca ye imman in: Quēn ōmitzmotlathuiltilì, quēn ōmitzmīxtōnaltilì in tlācatl in totēcuiyo in ilhuicahuà in tlālticpaquè, àço achìtzin ticmomàcēhuìtzinoa

The governor.

Oh my precious revered father, we are all fortunate that you inquire about us. The Giver of life, the divine God, is giving us too a bit of His day.

Addendum

The Indigenous *notary of the town greets a nobleman and judge.*

Oh personage, oh ruler, I (do not wish) you to take ill. I (do not wish to) give you stomach pains and disturb your lordship and rulership, to take you away from your food, to distract you, to make you forget about the governance of the city, for it is late. How did our Lord, the Master of heaven and earth, cause you to feel on rising? Are you enjoying a bit of His health, or is something of His afflictions and punishments

in ītēchicāhualiztzin; auh ànocè itlà mopantzinco quihuālmihuāliznequi in ītēmoxtzin in ièēcatzin in ītetzin in īquăuhtzin. Mā īxquich motlàpaltzin xoconmochīhuili tlācatle totēcuiyoe: Ca çan īxquich ic nocompachoa in momātzin in mocxitzin, ic nicnepechtēquilia in petlatl in icpalli.

R[a.]

Ōtiquìiyōhuì tlàcuilòtze, ōtinechmocnēlilì ca cencà nictlaçòcāmăti in motēcatlàtlaniliz in motēciauhquetzaliz: ca achìtzin nicnomàcēhuia in ȳtēchicāhualiztzin [f.13v] in totēcuiyo in īpalnemoāni: çan yèhuatl inīc ninàmana inīc ninocochìçoloa in itcōca in īmāmalōca in ātl in tĕpētl

Estos retazos de excelente Megicano son escritos por D[n.]*Miguel, Mr̂o del P. Oracio.*[*]

---

* Written in a different hand.

coming upon you? Be of good cheer, oh personage, oh our lord. This is all with which I kiss your hands and feet, with which I bow down to your authority.

Reply.

Greetings, oh scribe. Thank you. I greatly appreciate your inquiry and your greeting. I am enjoying a bit of the health of our Lord the Giver of life, but I am disturbed and losing sleep over the governance of the city.

These snippets of excellent Mexicano (Nahuatl) were written by don Miguel, aide to father Horacio.

GLOSSARY

Acolhua. An ethnic group living on the east side of the lake in the central basin of Mexico from at least the thirteenth century. Texcoco was the largest Acolhua altepetl.

Altepetl. A city-state in the Nahua world. An altepetl always consisted of smaller subunits, and it could also join with other altepetl to form a larger cooperatively governing entity.

Aztec. A word used today to refer to the people whom the invading Spaniards found in central Mexico. Sometimes it is used to refer to the Mexica specifically, and sometimes it refers to the Mexica and their close allies, including the people of Tlacopan and Texcoco. In this book, it has the latter meaning.

Huehuetlatolli. Ancient discourse, or words of the elders. An ornate rhetorical register of speech passed down through the generations.

Mexica. An ethnic group, including the people of Tenochtitlan and Tlatelolco. The Mexica are thought to have been the last migrants from the north to arrive in the central basin of Mexico.

Nahua. A speaker of the Nahuatl language.

Nahuatl. "Intelligible speech," a language in the Uto-Aztecan language family shared by the Aztecs and some of their neighbors that also served as a lingua franca in early Mexico. Today over a million people continue to speak Nahuatl.

Nezahualcoyotl. A powerful ruler of Texcoco who governed for approximately fifty years in the fifteenth century. He was the ancestor of the family featured in this text.

Nezahualpilli. A ruler of Texcoco who was the son of Nezahualcoyotl. He died shortly before the Spaniards arrived, and his many sons were still engaged in strife over the succession when the newcomers came.

Tenochtitlan. The great city of the Mexica, located on an island in the lake at the heart of the central

basin of Mexico. Today Mexico City sits where it once was.

Tepaneca. An ethnic group living on the west side of the lake in the central basin of Mexico from at least the thirteenth century. Azcapotzalco and Tlacopan were its two largest altepetl.

Triple Alliance. An informal union between three great altepetl in Mexico: Tenochtitlan, Tlacopan (of the Tepaneca), and Texcoco (of the Acolhua).

NOTES

Introduction

1 Commonly known to scholars in the field of Mesoamerican Studies as the "Bancroft Dialogues," this text is preserved in Special Collections of the Bancroft Library of the University of California, Berkeley. It is cataloged as Discursos Mexicanos: Huehuetlatolli, Ramírez Collection, BANC MSS, Mexican Manuscript 458.

2 The quotation is from Bernal Díaz del Castillo's engaging account of his participation in the expedition of Hernando Cortés, written in his declining years and published in later centuries. Díaz del Castillo, *Historia verdadera de la Conquista de la Nueva España* (Madrid: Biblioteca Castro, 2012), 448. The idea that Texcoco was the site of an especially rich production of art and music is associated with the

idea of Nezahualcoyotl as a Christian-like king and an artist himself, a notion heavily promulgated by Miguel Leōn-Portilla in such works as *Trece poets del mundo azteca* (Mexico City: UNAM, 1967). Both these works are available in English editions. However, Jongsoo Lee has recently demonstrated that the idea of Texcoco as somehow different from Tenochtitlan in this regard is a construction of modern times. Jongsoo Lee, *The Allure of Nezahualcoyotl: Pre-Hispanic History, Religion and Nahua Poetics* (Albuquerque: University of New Mexico Press, 2008).

3 A good introduction to the altepetl's early history is found in the opening section of Bradley Benton, *The Lords of Tetzcoco: The Transformation of Indigenous Rule in Postconquest Central Mexico* (New York: Cambridge University Press, 2017).

4 This history is often mischaracterized as a simple question of Tenochtitlan and Texcoco uniting to bring down Azcapotzalco. It wasn't nearly so simple: under normal circumstances, such a thing

would not have been possible. For a treatment of the complexities of what really happened, based on Nahuatl-language sources, see Camilla Townsend, *Fifth Sun: A New History of the Aztecs* (New York: Oxford University Press, 2019).

5 The child may have been as young as seven (sources differ). The point is that a mere boy became ruler because he had the backing of the current Mexica ruler, due to close kinship. See Townsend, *Fifth Sun*.

6 Camilla Townsend, "Polygyny and the Divided Altepetl: The Tetzcocan Key to Pre-conquest Nahua Politics," in *Texcoco: Prehispanic and Colonial Perspectives*, ed. Jongsee Lee and Galen Brokaw (Boulder: University Press of Colorado, 2014). The symbolic association of flowers with warriors is especially visible in the song lyrics known as the Cantares Mexicanos.

7 Over the course of the past generation, there has been excellent work done on the alacrity with which many Indigenous communities came to side with the

Spaniards. See, for instance, Laura Matthew and Michel Oudijk, eds., *Indian Conquistadors: Indigenous Allies in the Conquest of Mesoamerica* (Norman: University of Oklahoma Press, 2007). It is also true, however, that Nahuatl records demonstrate a great deal of uncertainty about what to do, and sometimes hostility toward the Spaniards greater than that directed at the Mexica. Cacama was one of the early Indigenous leaders to parlay with the Spaniards from his location in Tenochtitlan; the latter later turned against him and killed him. For an analysis of the actions of Coanacochtli, see Camilla Townsend, *Malintzin's Choices: An Indian Woman in the Conquest of Mexico* (Albuquerque: University of New Mexico Press, 2006), 129–31.

8 Díaz, *Historia verdadera*, 445.

9 Here spoke the well-known colonial writer, don Fernando de Alva Ixtlilxochitl. Translated in Amber Brian, Bradley Benton, and Pablo García Loaeza, eds., *The Native Conquistador: Alva Ixtlilxochitl's Account of the Conquest of New Spain* (Univer-

sity Park: The Pennsylvania State University Press, 2015), 59.

10 Peter Villella, "'For So Long the Memories of Men Cannot Contradict It': Nahua Patrimonial Restorations and the Law in Early New Spain," *Ethnohistory* 63, no. 4 (2016), 707–10. Villella's sources are papers of the Audiencia. For more on Ixtlilxochitl's efforts in the 1520s, based on Nahuatl-language testimonies, see Townsend, *Malintzin's Choices*, 130–32. Coanacochtli seems to have been killed along with Cuauhtemoc at Acalan along the route taken by Hernando Cortés to Honduras.

11 Careful analysis of textual references dates the manuscript to this period: see the Introduction to Frances Karttunen and James Lockhart, eds., *The Art of Nahuatl Speech: The Bancroft Dialogues* (Los Angeles: UCLA Latin American Center Publications, 1987), 7. On a broader level, James Lockhart brought to the field the concept of gradual acculturation as mirrored in evolving linguistic usages (linguistic "stages"). See James Lockhart, *The Nahuas after*

the Conquest (Stanford: Stanford University Press, 1992).

12 The book that launched the study of this important example of cross-cultural contact is Louise Burkhart, *The Slippery Earth: Nahua-Christian Moral Dialogue in Sixteenth-Century Mexico* (Tucson: University of Arizona Press, 1989). This rich field of study has continued to yield important work, including of religious texts written by Nahuas without the oversight of their Franciscan teachers. See, for instance, Ben Leeming, *Aztec Anti-Christ: Performing the Apocalypse in Early Colonial Mexico* (Boulder: University Press of Colorado Press, 2022).

13 Had Pablo himself been a student at the school, the text would have been far more Christianized. For a close comparison of certain paragraphs in the dialogues with material in Book 6 of the Florentine Codex, see Karttunen and Lockhart, *The Art of Nahuatl Speech*, 12–13. For a recent analysis of the remarkable Florentine Codex, see Jeannette Peterson and Keven Terraciano, eds., *The Florentine Codex:*

An Encyclopedia of the Nahua World in Sixteenth-Century Mexico (Austin: University of Texas Press, 2019).

14 They preferred to use the Roman alphabet to transcribe performances that in earlier days would have been memorialized in glyphs. See Celso Mendoza, "Scribal Culture, Indigenous Modes and Nahuatl-Language Sources," in *Oxford Research Encyclopedia of Latin American History* online, May 2020, https://oxfordre.com/latinamericanhistory/display/10.1093/acrefore/9780199366439.001.0001/acrefore-9780199366439-e-578.

15 For more on this subject, see Camilla Townsend, *Annals of Native America: How the Nahuas of Colonial Mexico Kept Their History Alive* (New York: Oxford University Press, 2017).

16 Recorded in Fernando Horcasitas, *The Aztecs Then and Now* (Mexico City: Minutiae Mexicana, 1979). More recently, anthropologists have taped similar exhortations. Personal communication from Jonathan Amith.

17 For examples taken from sixteenth-century documents, see Lockhart, *The Nahuas after the Conquest*, 120–21.

18 See Pedro Carrasco, "Royal Marriages in Ancient Mexico," in *Explorations in Ethnohistory: The Indians of Central Mexico in the Sixteenth Century*, ed. H. R. Harvey and Hans J. Prem (Albuquerque: University of New Mexico Press, 1984).

19 See Townsend, "Polygyny and the Divided Altepetl."

20 For more on the song tradition, see Peter Sorensen, "'I am a Singer, I Remember the Lords': History in the Sixteenth-Century Aztec Cantares" (PhD diss., Rutgers University, 2022).

21 For a study of the Franciscans in Mexico, see Steven Turley, *Franciscan Spirituality and Mission in New Spain, 1524–1599* (New York: Routledge, 2016), and an old classic, John Leddy Phelan, *The Millennial Kingdom of the Franciscans in the New World: A Study of the Writings of Geronimo de Mendieta* (Berkeley: University of California Press, 1956).

22 Debate exists as to whether the word means "ancient discourse" or "discourse of the elders." The grammar would indicate the former, but there are known usages where it clearly means the latter. James Lockhart was of two minds on the question. It is more than possible, even likely, that individuals in the sixteenth century themselves had different views of the matter.

23 In the 1530s and '40s, the Franciscan fray Andrés de Olmos transcribed some of the huehuetlatolli, but his original text does not survive. Olmos used some of his examples in his 1547 manuscript *Arte de la lengua mexicana*, several copies of which survive to the present day. (For an assessment of these, see Judith Maxwell and Craig Hanson, eds., *Of the Manners of Speaking that the Old Ones Had: The Metaphors of Andrés de Olmos in the TULAL Manuscript* [Salt Lake City: University of Utah Press, 1992], 10–11.) At the end of the century, another Franciscan friar, Juan Bautista Viseo, took Olmos's earlier text and published a heavily redacted

and embellished version, in line with Christian teachings (*Huehuetlahtolli, que contiene las platicas que los padres y las madres hicieron a sus hijos y a sus hijas* [Mexico City, 1600]). A good study of how the Franciscans wished to use the genre is Mónica Ruiz Bañuls, *El huehuetlatolli como discurso sincrético en el proceso evangelizador novohispano del siglo XVI* (Rome: Bulzoni Editore, 2009).

24 This paragraph is a distillation of the linguistic analysis done by Karttunen and Lockhart in *The Art of Nahuatl Speech*, 29–33.

25 In the last ten years, literally dozens of books with the word "gratitude" in the title have been released. School children are being asked to keep "gratitude journals" and the self-help literature for adults is replete with the concept.

26 At the end of the manuscript, there is a note explaining that "don Miguel" copied out the text for "father Horacio." Along the way, this don Miguel occasionally added parenthetical comments, indicating where he could not countenance a particular

grammatical formulation. Karttunen and Lockhart offer textual analysis demonstrating that father Horacio was most certainly the Jesuit scholar Horacio Carochi in their introduction to *The Art of Nahuatl Speech*, 2–6. Carochi's grammar—which includes some material from these dialogues—is available in English: Horacio Carochi, *Grammar of the Mexican Language*, ed. James Lockhart (Stanford: Stanford University Press, 2001).

27 In the 1860s, the French invaded Mexico and established a member of the Hapsburg royal family (Maximilian) as the "emperor" of Mexico. Certain conservative Mexicans had invited this development, hoping it would bring stability to their nation, but most of the people were against it, and they soundly defeated the French and their local allies within a few years.

28 The catalog for the sale of the Ramírez collection made the incorrect assumption that the "Huehuetlahtolli" among the holdings were the same as—or at least that the text was closely related to—the "Huehuetlahtolli" published by fray Juan Viseo in

1600. See note 23 above. That information has unfortunately made it into the Bancroft Library's catalog. However, the two texts are entirely unrelated.

29 Karttunen and Lockhart, *The Art of Nahuatl Speech*, 1–104 and appendices.

30 A good example of this would be fray Juan Viseo's *Huehuetlahtolli*, which offers Nahuatl-language dialogues extensively edited by a Franciscan pen. See note 23.

31 The Florentine Codex is an example of a text that is, on the one hand, invaluable, and yet on the other, riddled with places where it is clear that the orchestrating friar (in this case Bernardino de Sahagún) asked leading questions or even outright edited. The *xiuhpohualli*, or histories, are examples of texts that were produced without any involvement on the part of friars. They are a crucial source, but unfortunately, yield very little to nonexpert readers.

32 Karttunen and Lockhart, *The Art of Nahuatl Speech*, 67–100. Because of their diacritics, the Bancroft Dialogues were an important source for

Frances Karttunen's dictionary: *An Analytical Dictionary of Nahuatl* (Norman: University of Oklahoma Press, 1992 [1983]).

33 Karttunen and Lockhart, *The Art of Nahuatl Speech*, 170–99.

34 For classical Nahuatl, a reader might begin with James Lockhart, *Nahuatl as Written* (Stanford: Stanford University Press, 2002).

Part I. The Present

1 The subdivisions are generally insertions made in Spanish by an editor in the colonial period, possibly the assistant of father Horacio Carochi. These appear in italics. However, in the English translation, the editors of this edition have, for the sake of clarity, introduced some additional subdivisions as well as some additional words or phrases in existing subdivisions. These appear without italics.

2 It literally says, "I will disturb you," but the utterance (like all comparable ones throughout the text)

was clearly intended to be self-deprecatory. That is, the context, tone, and body language conveyed that the speaker did not wish to disturb.

3 It is likely that formal greetings had long begun with questions about health, but it is certainly true that the question had become increasingly central since the arrival of the Spaniards. Over the course of the century, Old World diseases caused nearly a 90 percent drop in the population. This text was written during the peak years of the population drop, as is mentioned by one of the speakers toward the end.

4 It literally says, "those who are afflicted" but the intended meaning is "us ordinary mortals." In the 1987 edition, Frances Karttunen and James Lockhart included two translations, a colloquial one and a more literal one. Only occasionally did they bring the literal expression into the colloquial translation. In this edition, we have brought a few more instances of the literal expressions into the colloquial translation. See the introduction.

5 This is a translation of "Ipalnemoani," literally meaning "the one through whom there is life," which was an epithet used in the preconquest era for the god Tezcatlipoca, and occasionally for other powerful deities. The Christian friars repurposed the term. For a foundational study on the interactions between the Nahuas and the Franciscans, see Louise Burkhart, *The Slippery Earth: Nahua-Christian Moral Dialogue in Sixteenth-Century Mexico* (Tucson: University of Arizona Press, 1989).

6 The idea that we have our loved ones only for a short time is also found with great frequency in the lyrics of the most traditional songs, which were likewise transcribed in the sixteenth century.

7 The idea that it was necessary to commit important acts "before the eyes of" important people or deities was very old and is found in many disparate texts.

8 These are old ways of saying, "Do not get yourself into trouble." The rabbit was associated with misfortune, the deer with brutish life out in the wild. The

idea that to live was to walk along a sort of balance beam between dangers is found in many sources.

9 Dirt floors must be kept slightly dampened in order to prevent dust from rising.

10 This strongly echoes older prayers to preconquest divinities, especially Tezcatlipoca. He mocked the efforts of mortals and delivered blows without warning.

11 Almost certainly the writer meant to put "you the mothers and you the fathers as he usually did."

12 It was understood that parents and grandparents struggled and sighed in their efforts to raise the next generation.

13 The speaker means to say that perhaps the marriage will result in the birth of children, who will carry the community forward.

14 The polite register in classical Nahuatl required certain reversals: a less powerful person would call a more powerful one his "son" or "nephew" and a more powerful person might call ordinary folk his "mothers and fathers." All of this plays out in the ensuing paragraph.

15 This was a classic pairing used to convey the idea of masculinity, and sometimes as a term for warriors. By the mid-sixteenth century, we occasionally find it used this way, as a term for a man who wishes to do right.

16 Once again, we see a polite reversal. The trained speaker is not really the governor's progenitor.

17 As in the paragraph above, the speaker is addressing Pablo using a polite form.

18 The references to what we have translated as "city" throughout this text are actually to the "altepetl," a key Nahuatl term conveying the notion of a community of people working together for the common good. It is often translated as "ethnic state" or "city state." The references in this text are often very poetic, but are difficult to translate adequately.

Part II. The Past

1 The writer means that one could place the name of any of several rulers here. This is further

proof that he had been exposed to the Florentine Codex (see the introduction), as this is a practice found in that work. There was regular intermarriage between various sub-altepetl of Texcoco and various sub-altepetl of Tenochtitlan in the preconquest period. See Pedro Carrasco, "Royal Marriages in Ancient Mexico," in *Explorations in Ethnohistory: The Indians of Central Mexico in the Sixteenth Century*, ed. H. R. Harvey and Hans J. Prem (Albuquerque: University of New Mexico Press, 1984).

2 This is rhetorical. Their home is in Tenochtitlan, but the messengers from Texcoco are saying in effect, "Our lord's home is your home." Similarly, when the Texcoco lord later speaks of Tenochtitlan as "our home" or "my home" he is indicating that he knows he is welcome there.

3 This was a common way of referring to the rulers of Tenochtitlan in the *xiuhpohualli*, or annals. The city was on an island in the midst of the great central lake.

4 The literal phrase is that "the heart has fallen [in a certain direction]." We cannot know from this distance in time if it indicated merely a fancy or a stronger feeling. References in the work of the seventeenth-century Nahua scholar Chimalpahin would indicate that, at least some of the time, strong feelings were understood to be in play. The "tuft and tassel" refers to the flowering of the corn plant: the young woman is being called the blossom of her family.

5 He means that he is asking not for concubinage, but for a true marriage, in which the young woman's children would be understood to have inheritance rights.

6 "Elder sister" was a metaphorical title for a lady who was to be the mother of the heirs.

7 This could be a figure of speech, but since the lord is not present, it is likely that the speakers call him this because he is in fact the nephew of the Tenochtitlan lord and lady being addressed. Earlier in the speech, the Texcoco prince has mentioned having his own origins in Atzacualco, a subsection of

Tenochtitlan. It would have been very likely that his mother was from there, as intermarriage was so common. Later, the girl's parents say very definitely that he is blood kin to them.

8 A preconquest title, literally meaning lord of lords.

9 The religion is this text is a mixture of precontact and post-contact. The idea of "an eternal home" is a translation of a Christian concept, but the idea that after death we go to a place where the flesh has been shaved away comes from much older motifs. In fact, much of the language echoes the lyrics of preconquest bereavement songs, especially the emphatic repetition that they will never again be able to see the beloved person who has died.

10 Once again, the speaker pairs the Christian idea of an "eternal home" with the classic Nahua metaphors for the place we all end up after death: without light or air, but also without troublesome fleas.

11 A central tenet of Nahua political life was that leaders were not to live in the lap of luxury and ease, but rather, to make all the people's problems their own problems. They were to go without sleep. Like parents, they were to spend their lives worrying about others.

Part III. Return to the Present

1 This man clearly has the role of a teacher or mentor to the boys. We cannot know the exact nature of his relationship to them.

2 The tutor is not really her progenitor. This is once again a polite way of addressing someone she values and to whom she is in debt.

3 It was common to refer to one's descendants as hair. The metaphor is undoubtedly connected to the idea of sprouting; in addition, it was notable to the Aztecs that hair did not decompose. One could save a lock of hair of a beloved person long after their death.

4 Most people who had been enslaved were women taken in battle. However, their children were born free and could even rise to be leaders of the community.

5 This section closely parallels in places the work of the mestizo friar Juan de Pomar, who was in fact from Texcoco. It seems that it was probably he who was copying parts of this text (or another closely related one), and not the other way around. For more on this subject, see Karttunen and Lockhart, *The Art of Nahuatl Speech*, 209–10.

6 This was a preconquest title for a chief's second-in-command, who held important spiritual duties.

7 The Nahuas did not have a word for "devil" or "demons" but the friars wished them to refer to their old gods as demons. Consulting together, the Franciscans and their Indigenous aides decided to use the word *tlacatecolotl*, a word for a malevolent owl-being that went about at night, as "demon." That is what the writer did here, in order to prop-

erly distance himself from his reference to the prior gods.

8 They lived in the time of Nezahualpilli. Every eighty days, they listened to a commemoration speech for the former ruler, Nezahualcoyotl. In that way they kept him—and the past—alive.

9 This was not merely a matter of sexual transgression. The backstory is central: when this happened, Axayacatl was no longer ruler of Tenochtitlan, and so his daughter was no longer important. The new king of Tenochtitlan (Moteuczoma) wanted his own daughter or niece to be the mother of Texcoco's heirs, the better to control them, and so he arranged to have the existing heirs destroyed.

10 We do not know exactly what this was, but it could have been a sort of hostel where merchants from Cholula could stay.

11 The ruler of Tenochtitlan had forced the Texcoco ruler to eliminate certain beloved heirs. He could at least humiliate the Mexica people by providing a grander public repast than they ever had.

12 For more on this dramatic tale, see Townsend, *Fifth Sun*, 80–83.

13 In this way, the destruction of the former heirs continued. See note 9 above.

14 This was a metaphorical way of referring to death.

15 The Aztecs called the non-sedentary peoples of the north "Chichimecs." They understood themselves to be descended of Chichimecs and held them in both awe and disdain at the same time. Here, it literally says the boy would run howling and shouting and "beating his hand against his mouth" as if he were a Chichimec. In short, he was trying to make a "savage" war whoop.

16 The implication seems to be that there might be an outsider or visitor who has come to eat with them.

17 This was a wall, broader at the base and narrow at the top, that marked their territory. The Spaniards saw it when they arrived, and were attacked when they crossed the boundary. This is an old song about the

past, not a creation of the colonial period. For more on the songs, see Sorensen, "'I am a Singer, I Remember the Lords.'"

18 By Nahua standards, the prior's response is so bare-bones as to be almost insulting (albeit unintentionally). The purpose of these dialogues was partly to train clergy, to make them aware of polite forms and help them avoid being the object of mirth. Horacio Carochi says quite directly in his grammar that if one does not attend to the subtle nuances of Nahuatl, one can be guilty of outright buffoonery.